THE POTENTIAL OF GOD'S PRESENCE

YOU WERE MADE TO SEEK & FIND THE FULLNESS OF GOD

JASON HEILMAN

The Potential of God's Presence
You Were Made to Seek & Find the Fullness of God

Jason Heilman

THE POTENTIAL OF GOD'S PRESENCE

ISBN 978-0-9847886-0-6

©2012 by Jason Heilman. All rights reserved. Except for brief excerpts for citation purposes, no part of this publication may be reproduced, saved in a retrieval system, or transmitted in any form or by any electronic, mechanical, photocopying, recording, or otherwise, without the permission of the editor, or under the terms of consensual agreement.

Printed in the United States of America

First Printing: January 2012

Unless otherwise noted, all scriptures are from the HOLY BIBLE: NEW INTERNATIONAL VERSION © 1973, 1978, 1984 International Bible Society. Used by permission of Zondervan Publishing House, All Rights Reserved.

Scriptures noted Message are taken from The Message by Eugene H. Peterson, © 1993, 1994, 1995, 2000, 2001, 2002. Used by permission of NavPress Publishing Group. All Rights Reserved.

Scripture quotations marked (KJV) are taken from the King James Version.

The author has added italics to quotations for emphasis.

Visit our website at www.jasonheilman.com

ENDORSEMENTS

It's not often that you find truly "fresh" perspectives from the Bible on long-standing major themes, such as worship. In your hands, however, through the skillful writing of Jason Heilman, you possess just such a treasure. "The Potential of God's Presence" is a treasure chest full of amazing concepts. This volume handles practical wisdom applicable to your daily, personal expression. Within these pages, Jason also expands understanding for you to gain greater freedom and prophetic insight during your corporate worship experience. Really, I can't say enough good things about this book, unlocking us "earthlings" to heavenly realms. This is a really good read for the soul and spirit.

John H. Parks
Pastor Freedom Fellowship Church Magnolia, TX
Regional Apostolic Director Antioch Oasis International

∞

I just got finished reading Jason Heilman's new book: The Potential of God's Presence, and I have to say that it resounded in me. Jason does a masterful job at relating his own life and journey as a leader and as a minstrel. Let me qualify for Jason: This book is not a worship guide for musicians but a hunger guide for the Body of Christ to really begin to open up to the fullness of what God has for us. Jason tells the principles that drive his own God story, then lays out a vision for us in the end of what he is dreaming of and you the reader will begin to dream the dream with him and heaven: that the Presence of God will fill the earth. Good job Jason!

Shawn Bolz
Director Expression58 Los Angeles, CA
Author Keys to Heaven's Economy
The Nonreligious Guide to Dating & Being Single
The Throne Room Company

A modern day psalmist and minstrel, Jason Heilman is a son of Shady Grove Church. When God first called Jason, he spent countless hours at the All Nations House of Prayer pouring out his heart to God. I remember the early days of walking past the prayer room as he worshipped before the Lord. He kept his hands on the keyboard and his heart before God, and God did a transforming work in his life. In his first book, The Potential of God's Presence, Jason shares the lessons he's learned since those early days and takes the reader on a journey to become a minister before God. The highest call on each of our lives is relationship with God - it is to know God and make Him known. Simply put, we are each called to minister to Him, to be a worshipper of Him. Jason challenges you to do just that. Allow The Potential of God's Presence to challenge you, move you, and encourage you as you answer the call to become a modern day psalmist unto God.

Olen Griffing
Founding Pastor Shady Grove Church Dallas, TX
Founder and Apostle Antioch Oasis International

∞

This book will motivate you to think and pray. It will cause you to laugh and cry and most of all, it will produce a desire in you to be more like Jesus and closer to Him.

Jon Dunn
Lead Pastor Shady Grove Church Dallas, TX

Jason has given the church an on-ramp for the presence of Jesus through his writing. A timely topic for EVERY BELIEVER, you will not be disappointed with The Potential of God's Presence! It will awaken your heart to all the possibilities of encountering God as you worship Him. Jason's writings will challenge you not to miss the relationship potential waiting for you as you set your heart apart to find Him. The Word is clear, God is looking for lovers, worshippers who will seek Him all their days. This book will provide a vital link in that quest. Happy reading!

Dr. Brian Simmons
Founding Pastor
Gateway Christian Fellowship West Haven, CT
Founder Apostolic Resource Center & Stairway Ministries

∞

When the church gathers, is it possible that God wants to do more in our midst than we experience? Might He want to far exceed our expectations and even break the box of our paradigms? There is no question that our Creator is perfecting His bride and making His Church into one without spot or wrinkle. God moving; we must follow. He is speaking; we must listen. Jason Heilman is on the leading edge of discerning this ecclesiological shift and we are privileged to glean from his insights in The Potential of God's Presence.

Josh Ellis
Senior Pastor New Life Church Petersburg, MI

Jason Heilman is a voice in the church today willing to challenge the traditions of man and promote a broader reality of the possibilities in God's presence. Jason has put language to the inner cry of a generation weary of tradition and longing for encounter with God. If you want to be challenged to a deeper place and are ready for a greater awareness of God's presence in YOUR life, start reading this book NOW!

Jamie Dickson
International Itinerant Minister
Founding Pastor Crave Ministries Waterville, ME

∞

Jason's new book is a must read for all those with a hunger for the fire of God's presence. As a true minstrel of the Lord, Jason puts words to the heart cry of a culture desiring to go beyond the potential trappings of religious tradition towards vibrant encounter with the living God. With a clear prophetic edge, Jason will challenge your current paradigms of the Western worship experience, and expand your vision for something more: communion with the heartbeat of heaven.

Michael Smith
Lead Pastor Ignite Church North Haven, CT

Dedication

To my daughter, Zoey Kulani Heilman,
and your generation….

May you dance with joy upon the revelations that
your mother and I have uncovered…

May our forerunnings be your normal…

Love, Daddy
Sunday, October 23, 2011 6:17PM

ACKNOWLEDGEMENTS

To my wife Ann-Marie, for your belief in me, this project and your support during the lengthy process of it's assimilation. I treasure and love you.

To Greg, Jeannie, Bets, Garren and my extended family, for supporting me in the things I've felt led to do by God in this life.

To Bill & Sherrie, for believing in your daughter's husband.

To Scott & Janina, for telling me it's crazy... and it's God!

To Olen, for generating a legacy that I've had the privilege of sharing in and now, for my part, carrying on.

To Gary & Norm, for your spiritual fatherhood in my life.

To Kim, for your mentoring that shaped me more than you know.

To Rayanna, for giving me a C in music theory and so much more.

To Marci, for your honesty that helped shape my words and my life.

To Bonnie, for being a source of inspiration.

To Paul, for making me a better writer.

To Clay, for making me a better musician.

To Jon & Lewis, for your open arms and continual support.

To **Welser**, for being the greatest servant I will ever know.

To **Dan, Tommy, Lex, Sebastian & Jake**, for joining me when nobody else would. And also, for your sweet skills.

To **Nic, Mike, Josh, Landon, Jamie & Brian**... Brothers don't shake hands, brothers hug.

To **Kevin**, for your service, willingness and deep talks over coffee.

To **Elias and the Modern Day crew,** what would we do without you?

To **Wayne & Dee,** your support will never be forgotten.

For the specific support of this project, special thanks go to my **Grandmother Betty, Wendy, Shawna, Ricardo & Drika, Larry, Becky, Norm & Paula, Phil & Melissa and Juan & Leigh Anne**. And to all those who, over the years, have sowed financially into what my wife and I do; We could not have done it without you.

                      Thank You All!

Table of Contents

About the Cover 15

Foreword 17

Introduction 19

Chapter One:
When You Seek Him You Will Find Him 25

Chapter Two:
God Desires Relationship 31

Chapter Three:
The Potential of God's Presence 53

Chapter Four:
Positioned for God's Presence 65

Chapter Five:
The Sound of God's Presence 89

Chapter Six:
Facilitating God's Presence 113

Chapter Seven:
My Journey as a Prophetic Minstrel 141

Chapter Eight:
The Minstrels - God's Atmosphere Creators 157

Chapter Nine:
The Ministry of the Minstrel 179

ABOUT THE COVER

God is willing to give as much of Himself as we purpose to receive. In my search for the book cover art, I felt as if this image of varied size glasses was an appropriate visual representation of this reality. Notice that, regardless of size, each glass is full. The size of glass is meant to depict our individual desire and chosen capacity for the presence of God in our lives. If your desire for God is a "small glass", He will fill that glass. He will fill your expectation. But what if there exists more than what you expect? What would occur if you decided to hold out a bigger glass?

Through this image and this writing, after all is read and done, my desire is to leave you with this simple exhortation…

"Consider a bigger glass."

FOREWORD

Let me say right off the bat that Jason's book is not just for worshipper leaders, but for all worshippers who desire to see the full measure of both the individual and corporate transformation that takes place in the cohesive combination of God's presence and His will. *"The Potential of God's Presence"* is more than just a book, it's a message for this and future generations.

I have known Jason as a friend and partner in ministry for many years now. I first met him while I was pastoring a church in West Texas. Jason and Ann-Marie came in to minister, and it was a powerful time. That weekend I realized Jason carries a unique anointing and ability to not only lead others in expressing their worship to Jesus, but to also lead them into atmospheres where they hear what Jesus is saying/singing to them. He is a true minstrel, declaring the heart of God in music and song. As a ministry leader myself, I would strongly encourage pastors and leaders to acquire several copies of this book to release amongst your congregation. I believe it will assist in expanding their understanding of their role in worship as well as increase their expectation level in God's presence.

I remember that as a child, sitting in many worship services and conferences during times of worship, I was thinking, *"So when does God get a chance to sing?"* Oftentimes worship services tend to be one song right after the other as we fill thirty-to-forty minute sets with as many songs as possible. God is still honored in that, but what if there is something that He wants to release in the midst of this? God is restoring that aspect of relational worship wherein we touch His heart and He touches ours. He sings over us and we sing back to Him. Jason Heilman is someone who is called as a conduit to "*bridge the gap*" of expression in the exchange between the Father and His children.

After reading The Potential of God's Presence, I can tell you that Jason has taken what God has revealed to him over many years regarding music, sound, worship, and the presence of God, and written it down in a practical, revelatory, and fresh way. If you desire to go beyond the ankle-deep waters of the river of God, Jason's book will encourage you and help take you into the deep waters where the full potential of God's presence is revealed. I know that you will enjoy this book as much as I did.

Nic Billman
Pastor, Worshipper Leader, Missionary
Director, Shores of Grace Ministries in Recife, Brazil
www.shoresofgrace.org

Introduction

There is a potential in the presence of God, and you were created to consistently walk in the awareness of Him. My desire is that this book be a catalyst for you, an inspiration that leads you into ever-expanding spirit encounters with the living God. I am a musician and minstrel with a passion to see people experience the vastness of the person, power and presence of God. The Bible tells us in Psalm 34, *"Taste and see that the Lord is good."* I believe that God has laid before every one of us the opportunity to consistently partake of the immense banqueting table of His character, nature and manifest presence. We simply need to understand how to continually make the most of this constant opportunity!

While we live in a world of natural laws and limitations, we were never meant to carry our association with a limited, natural world over into our relationship with an unlimited God. Endeavoring to encounter a fuller spectrum of God requires that we move beyond only seeking God with our finite minds and into a deeper understanding of how to encounter God spirit to Spirit.

In his letter to the Ephesian Church, the Apostle Paul prayed that they would know the love of Christ that surpasses knowledge (Ephesians 3:19). This leads me to propose the question, *"How can one know that which goes beyond knowing?"* The answer to this question lies in the fact that Paul knew that there was more than one kind of *"knowing."* There is a difference between knowing something in our minds versus knowing something in our spirits. Paul was telling the Ephesians that there are things of Christ that can be *"known"* which transcend what our finite minds can comprehend. There is unlimited potential in God for those that will pursue Him in the spirit.

The book of John, chapter four, tells the story of a woman's encounter with Jesus at a well. Jesus told this woman that those who desire to worship God, who is Spirit, must worship Him in spirit and in truth. It makes perfect sense that if we want to encounter God, who is Spirit, that we would engage God in relationship with our spirits. God gave each of us a spirit for the very purpose of connecting and staying connected with Him. God is even now searching for those that desire to both pursue and encounter Him in ways that go beyond the finite understanding of their minds.

While I believe that our minds and imaginations certainly can and do enhance our encounters with God, sometimes the finite mind is the very thing that limits us in our experiencing Him. Because they are finite, life tends to train our minds to perceive and believe that there are limitations upon everything. The finite mind often battles with the infinite spirit because the finite mind can't fully grasp that God contains no limitations. Our spirits, when aligned with the truth of God's Word, will influence and eventually take precedence over both our minds and bodies.

My desire and hope is to encourage you to pursue a continual spiritual awareness of the presence of God based upon a true understanding of the character and nature of Jesus Christ. An exciting life in the spirit awaits those who will tune in to His presence.

∞

If you are a person that would enjoy abiding more often in love, peace and joy, then you are a member of my target audience. Of course, the world has many ideas of how abiding in love, peace and joy should and can be achieved. My personal belief is that this is accomplished through abiding in a daily, relational, spiritual awareness of the person and presence of Jesus Christ. Well, one might say I just whittled my target audience down to a small minority. Not necessarily! I've never intended that this book be read only by Charismatics or any particular segment of the Christian Church or by only the Church, for that matter. If you already do have a relationship with Christ, I encourage you to read this and consider the exciting prospect of how much more there is to be discovered in God. If you don't consider yourself a "*Christian*" or even "*religious*," I'm asking you to read this book with the rumination that the person and presence of Jesus Christ is potentially the Source of the fullness of love, peace and joy, and that we can consistently abide in the awareness of His presence, and all that comes with it, if we will learn how to position and posture ourselves to remain in an awareness of Him.

∞

While writing to the Corinthian Church, the Apostle Paul mentioned the fact that we all see only in part and therefore can only prophesy in part (1 Corinthians 13:9). In essence Paul meant that nobody has all of the answers and that no one person can possibly begin to see the fullness of the big picture without the insight and perspective that God has also revealed to others. Before you even get to Chapter One, I want YOU to know THAT I KNOW that I don't hold all the answers. I'm sharing my perspective on the subject matter of this book's contents, and I'm simply asking you to consider the points that I am making. My hope is that your life will be enhanced by viewing some things from my perspective.

∞

I started writing this book because of my desire to help others expand their experiences into the depth, width and height of the presence of God. I believe that the vastness of God is infinite and that no matter where you've gone in God, there will always be more places to go. As a musician and worshipper leader, there have been instances when I've wanted to just stop in the middle of a time of worship to share information that would enhance people's experience. However, stopping in the middle of a song on Sunday morning to teach is not usually practical, nor appreciated by pastors for that matter. (I know. I've tried.) That's why I began to develop these writings in order to bring forth language that would reveal some enlightenment to the workings of the Spirit of God in the midst of musical atmospheres and that would suggest ways to practically discern and engage in the presence of the Lord. But what started as an idea for assisting people to enter into His presence during a worship meeting has evolved over these months and years of writing into a desire to exhort people to continually **be being** in the presence of God. And while I host corporate meetings and events that create these specific times of opportunity for people, I'm also of the mentality that if I can maintain an awareness of God's presence throughout my day that everything I do will manifest out of that awareness as worship. So, back to what I mean by be being in God's presence. It's the continual pursuit of developing a more consistent awareness of the person and presence of Jesus in our lives. I am on this journey and I'm sharing mine with you as an inspiration to you for your journey. I'm not a professional *"walker with Jesus."* I am not a master of the pursuit of Christ. I think that's why God gave us eternity to pursue Him because He knew that's how long we would need!

    I'm a musician. I love music and so naturally I'm biased in my belief that music is one way, if not the best way, to engage in an awareness of God. That being said, I want to acknowledge that the use of music is just one of many paths towards the awareness of God. But a large part of this book deals with ways that people can engage, both personally and corporately, into the presence of God through music/sound and proposes some ideas on how musicians and leaders in the church may facilitate others to enter into God's presence through the use of music and sound. I offer some thoughts on how to position and posture yourself before God for the purpose of tuning into His Word as well as how to release the fullness of what God has placed within you unto Him as your own unique form of worship. This life is an exciting spiritual journey with God in which we need never grow content with one form of pursuit, one manner of discovery or one style of expression as we continually relate to the person of Jesus Christ.

Jason Heilman

Chapter One
When You Seek Him You Will Find Him

It was Sunday morning and I was up on the schedule to lead worshippers into a heightened awareness of God's presence. I don't specifically remember much about the worship time that Sunday except that it was an incredible time in the presence of God. It's what happened after the worship time that I want to make reference to. One of the musicians on my team that morning, a guitarist with whom I normally did not play, came up to me after the worship time and, with a joyous look upon his face, excitedly proclaimed, *"Man, this morning was like CONFERENCE WORSHIP!"*

Later that day, I began to ponder what he'd experienced that morning that caused him to say what he'd said. The biggest question that I asked myself was, *"What's the difference between Sunday morning worship and conference worship?"* I understood that this man probably sensed something that Sunday morning that he did not usually sense on a *"normal Sunday."* He equated his experience that Sunday to experiences that he'd had during conferences in the past and obviously thought that his personal experience in worship that Sunday was on another level or *"conference level"* compared to a *"regular"* Sunday morning.

On more than one occasion I've pondered such thoughts as, *"Why do people seem to experience 'more' of God at conferences, events and 'revivals' anyway? Is there really such a thing as a **regular** time in the presence of God? Does God simply desire to manifest His presence more at conferences and special events than He does on Sunday mornings?"* If you look into the Word at what Jesus said about Himself, you realize that this mentality is totally contrary to His nature. Jesus said in Matthew 18:20, *"For where two* or three gather in my name, there am I with them." Jesus did not say, "When two gather in My name I'll show up in 50% of My glory, for a Sunday crowd 75%, and for the big conference I'll let it all hang out!" No, we must realize that every time we gather, 100% of the fullness of the potential of His glorious presence and dunamis power is available and in our midst. EVERY SINGLE TIME!

Please read what I am about to say understanding that I'm simply trying to convey a key that I've discovered in regards to engaging into the presence of God. Over the course of more than a decade of traveling and ministering in music, I've had people tell me that, during times when I had led them in worship, they seemed to be able to access realms in the presence of God that were more vast than what they were typically used to experiencing corporately. So for what purpose do I share this with you? While it's true that I've acquired musical skill and have been anointed by the Lord to play music, beyond creating a musical environment for people, my personal skill and anointing does not really matter **as it pertains to** people actually engaging in and accessing the presence of God. People may not always think about this, but ultimately their **decision** to access the presence of God is what got them into the presence of God. I can only create an atmosphere for people and encourage them to engage into what is available in the environment.

So let me tell you a major key that I have learned, and the probable reason why that man on my worship team told me that the Sunday worship was like conference worship: I've learned that when I seek the Lord with all my heart, I **WILL** find Him. **I've learned that, while there are many looking for a move of God, God is looking for a move of man, and that God will ALWAYS be there when I move towards Him.** It's not a maybe issue for me. The reason why people in an audience and even people on my team are able to enter into these places in God's presence with me is because they are coming into alignment with this attitude that I carry, that I WILL access the manifest presence of God. I treat a Sunday morning with three hundred people in the room the same way I do a gathering of 10,000 in the Philippines or a group of fifty at a Rejuvenation Gathering. I don't base my belief that God will or will not be with me based upon crowd size, circumstances or my surroundings. God shook a rat-infested jail cell when Paul and Silas worshipped (Acts 16:25-26). God was not compelled by the exterior conditions of the room but on the interior conditions of those men.

Something that was instrumental in shaping this attitude into my belief system took place on a missions trip I went on to Juarez, Mexico. Chuck and Ruth Babler, who had previously been missionaries to Africa, led the team. We had daily prayer meetings and worship as a team at our base before crossing the border into Mexico. At that time, I had not even been called as a prophetic minstrel/musician. Nobody on our team could even play an instrument, so most of the time we just sang a cappella. During worship one morning, Ruth came out of the kitchen with a jar of popcorn. Remember when popcorn came in jars and you popped it in pans? It was that kind of popcorn. She started shaking the clear jar of popcorn while she sang. Have you ever had that feeling when you were embarrassed for someone else? Not that it was justified, but that is how I felt in that moment. Hey, I was only 18 at the time! I remember just sitting there, not engaged at all in the time of worship. Later that day, Ruth said she wanted to talk to me. She had seen my reaction to her bringing the popcorn instrument out. She taught me a lesson that day, that it really didn't matter where you were or what instruments you had or did not have. What mattered was that you had God and that you could worship Him anytime, anywhere, under any circumstances.

What I want to shout from the rooftops is simple, that "*the odds*" for entering into the fullness of the manifest presence of God are ALWAYS 100%! When we truly come to understand and believe this, it will excite us and cause us to engage with God more often with more expectancy. And although God will continue to use the musicians and the teachers and the corporate gatherings, there is a presence of God that we can literally walk in every moment of our lives if we so desire to. And when we do come together corporately with this mentality, the synergy in a roomful of people that have grown to understand and practice this *"being with God"* on a continual basis will be explosive.

My desire is to release some perspective, insight and practical application on how we, both individually and corporately, might expand our understanding of and experience in the presence of the Lord. It's all about growing in an understanding of how to focus your spirit upon Jesus in the midst of the atmosphere and opportunity that you are surrounded by.

Worship is a Decision

Psalm 43:5 - *"Why, my soul, are you downcast? Why so disturbed within me? Put your hope in God, for I will yet praise him, my Savior and my God."*

Psalm 103:1 - *"Praise the Lord, my soul; all my inmost being, praise his holy name."*

It is my personal belief that if people would understand this one principle, that engaging into the worship and awareness of God is a decision, that it would increase the consistency, the manner and the fervor by which they worship and walk with the Lord. Getting into the presence of God rarely occurs *"by accident."*

One way I define worship is *"anything that you do in response to an awareness of the presence of God."* By *"do"*

I mean a number of things from singing a song, dancing a dance, sitting in silence to ministering to someone. But all of these actions first require that we make a choice to move our bodies, to release sounds with our vocal cords and to touch the lives of others.

As humans we are all made up of the three parts—body, soul and spirit. Jesus told the disciples that the spirit is willing but the flesh is weak (Matthew 26:41). Our desire to worship the Lord starts in the place of our spirits, and thus our spirits should dictate what our bodies and souls should do. I included a few passages from the Psalms of David at the beginning of this sub-chapter to draw your attention to something that David understood about his soul. The soul consists of our finite mind, will and emotions. When you read these scriptures, the reason why it seems like David was talking to his soul is because HE WAS. David literally spoke to his soul on more than one occasion and told it to praise the Lord. The part of David that spoke to his soul was his spirit, his spirit that was willing to enter in to the presence of God regardless of how he felt in body and soul.

So follow me into this scenario: *You're pulling into church, you had a bad drive over because the kids were fighting in the back seat and you are running late, again. You finally get into the sanctuary and the people are in the middle of the second praise song. People around you are clapping their hands with smiles on their faces, and you don't feel at all like any of these people look; you just don't feel like "entering in."*

This is just one of hundreds of possible scenarios we all face on a daily basis. But at moments like these, if we understand what David understood, we could literally enter into the presence of God within seconds. The understanding that your mind, will and emotions do not dictate *how* you will worship or *that* you will worship is invaluable, not just in the midst of a worship service, but in the journey of life. We can, like David, speak to our souls and our bodies and bring them into alignment with our willing spirits. Realize that YOU are more willing than you may have realized. You may have just been focusing more on the part of you that was unwilling. Your spirit continually longs for relationship with God in the courts of the Lord!

Chapter Two
God Desires Relationship

God the Father sent His Son Jesus to this earth to ultimately restore one thing: relationship. Songs, singing and music are only channels by which we engage God in living, vibrant relationship. Music can be used as a tool in order to sense what God is saying, to see who God is and to release our perceptions of Him back to Him as worship.

When I think about relationship with God, I immediately think about Adam in the Garden of Eden. I love the whole idea of walking with God in the midst of the creation that He made for me to enjoy Him in. I enjoy getting away with God in nature as I always have. When Adam and Eve were tempted to eat of the tree of the knowledge of good and evil, I believe that this was the beginning of man's battle with distraction. Now, in our current age, there are more things available to distract us from the perception of God then there have ever been in all of history. Although I love the tech age that we live in, I think that technology is potentially one of the biggest distractions from the perception of God that we all have to deal with.

I am thankful for the fact that God sent Jesus Christ to make the way for all of us to have access to the presence of God. But, you can know this all day long and still not enter in to the presence of God. Although we have already been given access into the presence of God, many distractions surround us every day that keep us from engaging in the continual perception of God.

I believe that God desires to both speak to us and hear from us on a continual basis. It's a blessing to realize that God has songs to sing over us and revelation to speak to us. Listening is just as much part of the *"Worship Experience"* as our outward expressions are, whether that be singing, dancing or other expressions.

I know many of you have experienced what I call a glimpse into the heart of the Father God. It's the honor of experiencing the thoughts and feelings of the Creator of the Universe. On more than one occasion the Lord has taken me to the place where He has shared His heart with me. During times of historical study, God has literally taken me to places in history in which He had experienced the relationship with man that He desires. The Garden of Eden is one. Another is the Tabernacle of David.

When I talk about the fact that God showed me these places in history, it was not just simply that I read a historical account of something. It's always more than that. God will show me in the Word the history of the Tabernacle of David, but then He will share His longings, emotions and even memories attached to this history. I felt God was saying directly to me, *"Jason, I am looking again for the relationship and the expressions of My people that I once experienced during the time of David's Tabernacle. Even now, I desire people to know that there is no longer a veil between Me and them. I am longing for the intimacy with My children now like I had then. I miss the sounds and movements of freedom that sprang forth from those worshippers."* Of course, I am simply trying to share in words the impressions that I received in my heart. My experience is usually more like an impression, as if God is letting me in on His thoughts and feelings.

I have also experienced this when I've studied about the beginning of the New Testament Church. There was a freedom and creativity of expression in those days that people had, before the institutionalization of the church. God shared with me how He desires to hear the songs of His children. He does not necessarily miss a specific song, but a sound, and it's the sound of His children releasing their spontaneous, made-up songs and sounds to Him.

How Did the Church Lose Their Song?

The New Testament Church started out quite spontaneously. People were going from house to house sharing meals and encouraging each other. Acts 2:46-47 states: *"Every day they continued to meet together in the temple courts. They broke bread in their homes and ate together with glad and sincere hearts, praising God and enjoying the favor of all the people. And the Lord added to their number daily those who were being saved."*

I personally enjoy the simplicity that I find by which the church had fellowship in those early years. They enjoyed meeting with each other to both worship God and share with each other what the Lord was saying back to each of them. A true joy surrounded the lives of these early believers, a true and vibrant by-product of hearing and receiving the Good News of the Kingdom.

Even in the midst of persecution, this form of fellowship thrived for the greater part of the first three centuries. In the book, *The Oxford History of Christian Worship*, Geoffrey Wainwright describes this early period of the church:

"Solo singing by musically gifted members of the gathered church is the most clearly attested musical role during the first three centuries of the church. The earliest reports from the New Testament and from the second and third centuries suggest that singing was most common at meals, whether eucharist or agape. Among the very slender evidence, Paul's first letter to the Corinthians stands out for its description of urban worship in the first century. He lists singing among a number of worship practices that individuals spontaneously offered to the assembly during the course of worship. In a passage from the early third century, Tertullian (c.170–225) describes similar practices at the Agape meal: 'After the washing of hands and the lighting of lamps each

is urged to come into the middle and sing to God, either from the sacred scriptures or from his own invention." [1]

In the midst of my research and study, the phrase quoted by Tertullian, *"from his own invention,"* really struck me. In the midst of Christian fellowship, people were basically encouraged to get into the middle of a circle and sing their own spontaneous song to the Lord. It was a song from the heart, a response to the Lord. These songs were deemed to be in order because the atmosphere that was created allowed people to release their spontaneous songs. These songs were edifying because the others listened to the expression of the singer and took in the revelation of what they were releasing into their own spirits. It indefinitely created a chain reaction of praise by which many would release their songs unto the Lord. In those days, creativity in worship was encouraged.

Over time, a shift away from this freedom and creativity began to occur. Clement of Alexandria condemned the use of musical instruments in worship because of their use in pagan rituals. This controversy began as early as the latter part of the second century. In essence, Clement released what God intended to be used for worship to the world. He was not able to understand that instruments are essentially neutral and that the intentions of the musicians were what mattered.

In the year 313 AD, *The Edict of Milan* was a letter signed by emperors Constantine and Licinius that proclaimed religious toleration in the Roman Empire. This was great news for those that had experienced persecution because of their faith in Christ. The bondage of persecution was beginning to wane. But, in the midst of these changes, a new bondage was on the horizon, the bondage of restrictive liturgy.

A shift would begin to take place within the advent of organized religion that would be the beginning of a repression within the individual Christian's expression that would last, in this context, for 1,000 years.

Let's look again to *The Oxford History of Christian Worship* for more insight into this period of change within the organized church.

> "Commentators from the fourth century onward mention unison singing as expressing symphonia (sounding together, i.e., acclamatory agreement) and the distribution of musical roles and the structure of music itself were considered to express harmonia (the right relationship of parts to a whole). As stated by Clement of Alexandria, the whole Church could be characterized as being in harmony with Christ: "The union of many, which the divine harmony has called forth out of a medley of sounds and division, becomes one symphony, following the one leader of the choir and teacher, the Word, resting in the same truth and crying out: 'Abba Father'". These core musical metaphors were also used to reflect on existing musical practices in order to demonstrate how they supported proper organization of the Church's ministry. **From this perspective, the early church's charismatic solo song, which seems to have emerged as a way of expressing the uniqueness of the new faith, needed to be properly integrated into the service.** As Paul's letter to the Corinthians makes clear, such offerings needed to be edifying in order to be in correct relationship (harmony) with the church. The fourth- and fifth-century emergence of the lector chant with congregational response seems to have signified a particularly important balance, since the unity singing of the response by the solo singing of the lector could be interpreted as ordering both soloist and congregation into a musical harmony centered upon listening and responding to scripture." [2]

In other words, the institutional church wanted to take away the unique expression of one's response to their faith in Christ for the purpose of fitting it into their service order! Eventually, the church clergy ended up becoming the source of the congregation's response rather than the individual's response to God's direct, revelatory presence.

The church thought that edification could only come to people if it was controlled directly by a certain leader. Responses were no longer released as a result of direct inspiration but out of participation in a religious act. It seems that the church meant well, but it ended up squelching the unique, creative expressions of the church to its Creator. The church leaders of that day misunderstood what the Apostle Paul meant by *"decently and in good order."* (1 Cor 14:40) Paul never intended that the expressions of the individual Christian be completely discarded for the sake of some *"holy harmonia."* I don't believe it was ever God's intent that the individual expression of each one's praise should be silenced for the purpose of a collective, joint expression dictated by a clergy. But this is precisely what began to happen during this period.

Fear: A Source of Institutionalism

When you look back in history, one of the major reasons the church was institutionalized was because of a fear of both persecution and heresy. Institutionalism arose as a means of defense against persecution from the state and imposition of error from heretical sects such as Gnosticism. Reacting to these threats, the church formalized worship and centralized power in the bishop. Instead of choosing to take the time to teach and disciple people, the church decided to put one person in charge in order that he may keep *"order"* within the church. Eventually, as the bishop and clergy began to dominate the life and ministry of the church, the prevalence and influence of spiritual gifts within the individual diminished.

Ignatius, a church leader in the early part of the second century, was one of the first that seemed preoccupied with promoting and defending the authority and prestige of the bishop. He said that you could not have a love feast or gathering without the bishop. He stated that if the Eucharist was not performed by the bishop that is was invalid. In one of his writings he even stated that you should, *"do nothing without the bishop."* Can you imagine someone telling you that your worship in your car on the way to work was invalid because your pastor was not in the passenger's seat with you? That was how extreme Ignatius was. The thoughts introduced by Ignatius led to the development of the medieval Roman Catholic Church and its monarchial bishop. Church forms of both office and ritual came to be valued over personal, spiritual experiences. This also meant that spontaneous manifestations of the Holy Spirit became less desirable, especially by those in authority.

When Jesus walked with the disciples, He encouraged them to step out in faith. There were many times that the disciples failed, but Jesus stuck with them. Jesus' answer to the disciples' mistakes was continued discipleship and relationship. Acts 4:13 states, *"When they saw the courage of Peter and John and realized that they were unschooled, ordinary men, they were astonished and they took note that these men had been with Jesus."* In this Scripture, we see the results of the time that Jesus took with these men. The moving of the disciples in signs, wonders and miracles in the Book of Acts is the result of discipleship, relationship and the loving rebukes we find in Matthew, Mark, Luke and John. The example that Jesus shows us of discipleship reveals that it is not always a perfect process. In one moment you might find Jesus calling Peter a rock, the next you might find Him rebuking Peter for the dumb thing he just said.

It seems that the church adopted institutionalism in order that they would not have to deal with the issues that came along with true, biblical discipleship. Instead of having to deal with someone in the church that might sing a song or speak a prophetic word that may need a little correction, why not just silence the people altogether!

Concern with the Prophetic Ministry in the Church Today

"Jason, I would love to have you minister to the church. I just don't think my pastor would be cool with letting you sing prophetically, though." I can still remember talking to my worship pastor friend on the phone as we discussed the possibility of me coming to minister at his church. Of course, my friend would have loved to have me, but the pastor was another story. My friend went on to tell me that his pastor would not want me to sing prophetically during the worship service, but that he would rather have me just sing a list of worship songs. I told my friend that I understood, but it led me to ask the question, *"What is this particular pastor concerned about?"*

Revelation 19:10b states: *"For the testimony of Jesus is the spirit of prophecy."* Prophecy in its most basic form is for the comfort, encouragement and edification of the church. When I look at this verse in Revelation, it speaks to me that the very things that are on the heart of Jesus are those things that breathe forth the prophetic words that we, as his representatives, speak. With this thought in mind, not only do I believe that the prophetic has a place in the church today, I also believe that each believer should be moving in the prophetic.

So why is there a current concern over the moving of the prophetic in many churches today? I believe this concern has a lot more to do with the method by which God's word goes forth than it does the actual encouragement. The possibility exists that people might be confused or offended by spontaneous encouragement from the people of God to the people of God through someone other than a pastor. I know that the prophetic ministry has not been administered correctly in recent church history, but we simply can't throw out a valid ministry because of past misuse. I will admit that dismissing the prophetic entirely is one way to avoid the problems that are often associated with its misuse. But what might we possibly miss out on by dismissing the prophetic?

I believe that the best way for people to avoid confusion with the prophetic is to teach people how to function in and receive from the gifts of the Spirit. This will yield a people equipped with discernment of the prophetic, not just within one church, but also in the context of everything they will face throughout their lives.

The reality of the prophetic music ministry that I've released over the years is that people all around the globe have been encouraged and blessed. The way that I play music and release the Word is not what I or others would call typical. There are some pastors who don't have an issue with this at all. In fact, they quite enjoy it. There are other pastors and leaders, like my friend's pastor in the story above that might. Does the fact that this pastor does not embrace the prophetic negate my ministry? Absolutely not, because I have history and fruit that show that the prophetic music ministry brings encouragement and life to people. My point here is that I don't believe dismissing the prophetic ministry entirely is the answer to the concerns with the prophetic ministry in the church today. If I actually had the chance to sit down with my friend's pastor, I would tell him that I desire to see people understand how to discern and receive from the Lord through the prophetic. I believe it's worth it to take the time to help people understand how the prophetic works, how we can release it and how we can receive from it.

Tehillah "Homemade" Praise

Have you ever seen a picture created by a child hung upon a refrigerator door by a proud parent? Crayons form scribble marks accompanied by signatures with backwards letters. Often times you have no idea what the picture even is. But to a parent, this is of no importance. The art was proudly displayed, not because of the professionalism of display. It was simply displayed because it came from their child. In reality, the form of the creation was not the issue, but it was the fact that their child even took the time to create a drawing for them.

My mom still has stuff I made for her when I was a kid. I remember making a clay pot in sixth grade art class for her. This clay pot is the saddest looking clay pot ever made. It is all contorted and out of shape. But to this day, when I go over to visit my parents, I see this little blue pot sitting by the kitchen sink in their house. My mom uses it for her soap dish. I know for a fact that she does not use it for her soap dish because of the beauty and quality of it. She still has it because every time she looks at it, she remembers the day her little kid came home from school and gave it to her. Some of you know where I'm going with this, but let me give you another one.

One of the things my wife will always remember is when I sang a song that I wrote for her at our wedding. I originally presented the song to her when I asked her to marry me. Now, I could have chosen to sing a popular love song written by a famous entertainer in the music industry. But I chose to take the time to compose and write an original creation. I knew what I was doing! If I had sung a song written by someone else, that would have been nice. But the song I wrote for my wife is her special song from me. That song will never be sung by anyone else for anyone else. I will never sing that song to anyone else, because I created it for her alone.

She can treasure this song in her heart for the rest of our lives as her very own. Women don't want to hear fancy, recycled one-liners from their man. They want you to tell them what you think about them. They want you to look at them physically and inwardly and convey, with words, the beauty that you see.

In my relationship with my wife, I have refused to let Hallmark do my work for me. I enjoy coming up with my own creative words that express how I love and appreciate my wife. One of our favorites came with the inclusion of a well-known donut chain. If any of you have heard of Krispy Kream Donuts, you will understand what I am about to tell you. This donut shop has a sign on it that lights up when the donuts are coming fresh out of the oven. The sign reads in a bright red, neon glow, "*Hot Now!*" If you have never had a hot, freshly glazed donut before, let me just tell you it is a beautiful thing! The story goes that I was driving with my wife and we passed by a Krispy Kream that happened to have their "*Hot Now*" sign on. All of a sudden, it just popped in my head and I looked at my wife and exclaimed, *"If you were a Krispy Kream donut shop, your HOT NOW sign would ALWAYS be on!"* Needless to say, my wife loved it. Even to this day, when we pass a donut shop, we laugh in remembrance of this. I share this humorous story to help you realize that God is similar to us in that He also loves originality. He created us in His image to be creative as He is creative. I believe that our creativity should also extend to the way that we worship Him. Imagine with me now that God has a gigantic refrigerator in heaven. He is waiting to fill it with the homemade expressions of His children's praise. This *"homemade praise"* is known in the Word of God as Tehillah praise. There are many different words for praise in the Bible, each describing varying expressions and forms of praise. Here I want to focus on the Tehillah. Psalm 22:3: *"But thou art holy, O thou that inhabits the praises of Israel."* (KJV)

In this verse, the word for praise in the original Hebrew language is *"Tehillah."* Tehillah is defined as *"A spontaneous new song. Singing from a melody in your heart by adding words to it. This refers to a special kind of singing — it is singing unprepared, unrehearsed songs. Singing straight to God."*[3] According to this Scripture, Tehillah is the praise that God inhabits. In making such a statement, it is really important for us to look into what the word *"inhabits"* means in the context of this scripture. The original Hebrew word for inhabit in this scripture is *"yashab"* (yaw-shab'). It means to sit down, to dwell, to remain, to marry, to tarry. [4]

Before I say anything else, I want to say that I believe that God is always amongst us. He is the omnipresent God. He is everywhere all the time. That being said, just because He is always there does not always mean that people are aware of it. Have you ever been told by someone that they saw you at a mall or restaurant even though you never saw them? They were in the same place you were, but you never came into the awareness of their presence. This happens all the time in our lives as it relates to the presence of God.

God is always in the midst of all of us. I believe that when we begin to sense the presence of God in our midst, it is not that God has arrived, but that we have! We have arrived at the realization of His presence. How many times have we welcomed God into our presence when the truth is God has already given us a permanent invitation into His?

The word says in Jeremiah 29: *"When we seek Him, we will find Him when we seek Him with all of our hearts."* I believe that God is always amongst us, but it's up to us how often we truly engage into a relational awareness of God. God is on constant stand-by, always ready to engage in relationship with His children. The manifest presence of God is simply the omnipresence of God that people have chosen to embrace.

The other day I had a humorous, analogous thought

of how this related to Clark Kent and Superman. Clark Kent is the guy that always seems to be around, but not many people notice him. But, when someone starts crying out for help, Clark Kent runs to the phone booth and transforms into Superman. When you think about it, Clark Kent is always Superman. He always has the ability to fly and manifest superhuman strength, but it is the cries of people that motivate Clark Kent to transform and manifest into Superman. In a related way, when we call out to God, He moves from His omnipresent Clark Kent-like state into His manifest–present, Superman-like state, and He starts moving in the fullness of who He is.

So, getting back to the Tehillah: I believe this is the cry of praise that moves God to manifest Himself among us in ways that go beyond His general omnipresence. This point is proven true through the life of Jesus when He walked the earth. The Bible says that Jesus did not do many miracles in His hometown because of the people's unbelief (Mark 6:4-6). Just because Jesus was in the town did not automatically mean that miracles were taking place. There was a difference between Jesus being in a geographical location and the manifest, powerful presence that Jesus displayed in locations throughout His ministry. God said that those that would find Him would be those that were purposefully looking for and seeking after Him. Many of the miracles that took place in the Gospels came as a result of men and women who cried out for and pursued the person, presence and power of Christ. What if the woman with the issue of blood would have stayed home on the day Jesus came to her town? What if the blind man would have not cried out for the Son of David to have mercy upon him?

God Rules and Manifests from Your Tehillah Throne

While ministering to the Lord in a house of prayer, I became overwhelmed with a deeper understanding of Jesus, the Prince of Peace. I pictured Jesus sitting upon a throne, ruling as the Prince of Peace, but not just any peace. It was MY peace! The Lord revealed to me that He wants to shift the rulership of people's peace from other things back to Him. There are many people whose peace is not being ruled by Jesus. Their peace is being ruled by the economy, society, personal circumstance and the media. As I began to exalt the Lord and worship Him as the Prince of Peace, I literally felt a shift occur within me and I was overwhelmed with the peace of Christ. I believe that the Lord manifested His peace into my being because I built Him a throne of praise from which He manifested His peace to me.

When I began to understand the fact that God literally enthrones Himself upon my Tehillah Praise, it changed the way I approach the Lord. The Lord recently spoke to me, *"Jason, I don't enthrone myself upon the complaints, worries, fears or doubts of my people. I enthrone myself upon the Tehillah Praises of my people."* What God began to reveal to me is that He really wants to manifest in my life, but that He asks me to actually build, with my Tehillah, the throne from which He will rule and manifest in my personal life.

I've come to a place where I have stopped asking Jesus to give me that which He's told me He's already given. When I have a need, I seek the aspect of the character of God that meets my need and I build a throne of praise for the Lord according to that aspect of who He is. This causes me to eventually line up with the reality of God's Kingdom and His Word. Let me mention that I'm not giving you a magic formula to get God to give you whatever you want. But, since I've been moving in this revelation, I have begun to experience the manifestation of God and His Word in a greater consistency than I've ever experienced. The consistency is not due to the fact that God finally *"woke up"*; I believe it's because I have discovered an important key in accessing the presence and power of God through my Tehillah Praise.

God wants to establish His rule within us. He wants us to flow in a continual understanding and revelation of who He is. The way that this rule stays established is through our continual discovery and praise of God. As I continually praise, that reality of God continues to remain established in my heart. When we let worry and doubt creep in, *"false thrones"* begin to be established in places that are meant for the truth of God and His Word. God wants to rule, reign and manifest in our lives. He wants to be our Prince of Peace. He desires to rule and reign in our hearts.

God's Honor — Man's Distraction

God responds to the cries of His people. He is not interested in how professional your cry sounds. Recently I was leading worshippers in a church and we began to move into a time of spontaneous praise. All I was doing was playing music and creating an atmosphere for the people to praise God from their hearts. One woman began to cry out to the Lord. She was doing it quite loudly and demonstratively and I noticed some people kind of began to look over at her. I was instantly reminded of the woman who washed the feet of Jesus with her hair and poured the expensive perfume upon Him (Luke 7:38). Some of the people in that room thought of this woman as a distraction. Jesus received her worship as a great honor. I was not about to allow people to think that the woman in the worship service, who was genuinely crying out to God in thanks, was a distraction. In fact, I encouraged others to enter into their own Tehillah.

Some might have said that this woman was out of order. They said the same thing about the woman who washed the feet of Christ. But I, as a leader, was creating a neutral atmosphere for people to worship the Lord with their Tehillah. So, in reality, this woman was in complete order. She was doing exactly what the atmosphere had been set for. She was moving within the confines of what leadership had set in place for her. I think it's very important to allow people to release the songs and expressions that are uniquely theirs.

Consider with me that what is acceptable to God is not necessarily what always looks good to men. When four men ripped the roof off of a house and lowered a lame man into the room to Jesus, that sure didn't look professional. But he got to Jesus, and Jesus knew that anyone who was willing to rip the roof off of a house to get to Him must have some faith. Jesus forgave their sins, and the man eventually was healed (Mark 2:3-12).

As a worshipper leader, I don't ever want to confine people to a form in which they are unable to go after God in the way that they may need to. Some may be content on Sunday with the songs that we sing, and that is fine. But I always want to present people with a neutral atmosphere in which they can seek after and find God in a way that meets their specific need in the moment. I am aware that the Holy Spirit teaches and knows all things and that not everyone is going to receive what they need in the confines of the lyrics of the songs that I have chosen for that particular service. People showing up are going through the stuff of life and they may need more than to sing a few songs, they may need to Tehillah their way into the manifest presence of God to obtain and walk in their Kingdom inheritance which is in Christ. It's not every Sunday that they may need to *"rip the roof off,"* but if someone needs to in any given time, I want to give them that chance. I am not there to dictate how they encounter God; I am there to serve them in order that they may personally encounter Him to receive the *"now"* word that they need.

There's No Other Praise Like Your Praise

When I look at the Bible in a broad, all-encompassing way, I see it as a love story between a Father, Son and the Son's Bride. It is a true story, the story of the creation of man, the fall of man and the redemption of man through the blood of the Son. God created us for relationship with Himself. The Father desires a Bride for His Son, and we, the Church, are the collective expression of the Bride of Christ. When all is said and done, all of those that have acknowledged Jesus as their Lord and Savior throughout history will be brought together as one to be presented as a Bride for the Son of God. This collective Bride will be the result of the sum of many parts. Each of us, as individuals, will be a piece of the collective Bride. There will be an expression within the Bride that comes from every nation, tribe and tongue.

That said, we, as individuals, need to realize that no part of this bride is any more valuable than another. We are all important. In First Corinthians 12, Paul talks about the importance of the entire Body of Christ. In verse 27, he states, *"Now you are the body of Christ, and each one of you is a part of it."* Throughout this theme, Paul points out that each member of the body is both important to the body itself as well as to God. Verse 18 says, *"But in fact God has arranged the parts in the body, every one of them, just as He wanted them to be."* We have to realize that God has created each of us specifically the way that He wanted us to be. There is something unique concerning each of us that is unlike anyone else on the face of the earth. There never has been and never will be anyone else like you.

When it comes to worship, each of us has a unique expression that God desires, something that each of us alone can give Him. When you really think about this, it should create an excitement within you! You have something to give God that nobody else in all of history has been able to give Him: Your Song! Science has even discovered that each individual's DNA produces a unique pattern or song. Genetic music is generated by decoding and transcribing genetic information within a DNA sequence into a musical signal having melody and harmony.[5] Science is even now beginning to show us that we are uniquely created by a Creator with a purpose and expression within each of us that is specifically our own.

Recently, as I was seeking the Lord on these things, the Lord impressed upon my heart how He longs to hear the songs of His children. God desires to hear every one of the individual expressions of each of His uniquely created children. I believe that many of these songs and expressions have been lost and continue to be lost in the midst of modern Christian culture and church liturgy. History shows us that the unique worship of the individual Christian has been under assault since Pentecost. Many early Christians were persecuted and martyred for their faith in Christ. And, after Christian persecution was widely ended in the early fourth century, the Christian's individual expression of worship was again quenched by the ordinance of a controlling church clergy accompanied by a restrictive liturgy.

It is clear in Scripture that Jesus longs to hear the song of His beloved bride. Like many scholars, I believe that the Song of Songs is an allegory that parallels Christ's relationship to us. One of my favorite portions of Scripture comes out of Song of Songs chapter 2. Burning with love, the lover beckons his beloved in verse 14, *"Let me see your face, let me hear your voice, for your voice is sweet and your face is beautiful."* God created us in His image and likeness. We are uniquely formed to love, just as our Maker loves. I believe Jesus continues to call out to each one of us, calling us out of our hiding places in order that we may release our unique song and sound to Him.

The Restoration of Creativity is for the Entire Church

There is an obvious creative element involved in the *performing arts*. That being said, creativity being restored to the church is not only for the performing artists, but for the individual worshipper as well. Here I personally define performing arts as those done on a stage to be viewed by others. The performing arts are utilized to minister revelation to others through their various forms. I draw attention to this difference because if people that are not called to the performing arts limit creativity to only the performing artists, it might possibly halt them in the creativity of their personal worship to the Lord.

For example, there is a difference between a church having a dance team versus seeing a people being released in dance within the congregation in a non-professional, non-performance way. If a church gets a word for the restoration of the arts, they may put together a dance team and think that's the fullness of restoration, but it's only part of the restoration.

I believe God desires entire congregations of people to understand how to release their worship in creative, artistic ways. Performance art is great and can be used as a tool to impart the heart of God to people. What I'm talking about here is seeing creativity restored to the WORSHIPPER so that God may receive a full spectrum of worship from His children.

My wife has heard it before, "*If I could dance like you dance then I would dance too!*" I've heard it myself, "*If I could sing like you, then I would too.*" Please understand that I am trying to encourage you and the church to realize that the Father God longs for your expression, not because it is professional by man's standard, but because it's from you. Ask God for a greater level of His joyous perspective of your individual worship. This perspective will change your life! My prayer is that more and more people would begin to transition from being only observers of art to creators of it.

The "New Sound" Is Now

For years I've heard different people talking about a *"new sound"* that is coming from Heaven to the Church. It's supposedly going to be a sound from Heaven that God will sovereignly reveal to a generation so that they can use this sound to draw people's attention to the Lord. When I sought the Lord regarding this, I felt Him impress to me that, *"The New Sound Is Now. Whenever you release a sound of spontaneous praise from your heart, that is THE NEW SOUND."*

My view of the *"new sound"* is that it's not one that will be discovered by a special individual or band to be broadcast to the masses. I believe that this new sound will be discovered by individuals and that this sound is already resident within each of us. I believe that our new sounds will be released in conjunction with new discoveries that we find in God. A new daily discovery will release a new daily sound, a sound of spontaneous, homemade praise unto the Father.

One thing you have to realize is that, regardless of whether or not you hear it, sound is still sound. Many of you have heard the question, *"If a tree falls in the forest and no one is around to hear it, does it still make a sound?"* My answer is that it still makes a vibration. Just because you are not there to receive the vibration does not mean that one was not released. Relatedly, subsonic and ultrasonic sounds are still sounds even though they exist outside of the realms that our ears can perceive them.

Having said this, I believe that some of the sounds that God releases won't even be heard by our ears. There are sounds God wants us to receive with our spirits. We can't limit the sounds that God is releasing to those which are available to our auditory senses.

There is also the issue of what one defines as *"new."* What is new to one person may not be new to someone else. I sing worship songs that are so old that young people think they are new because they were not even born when the song was originally released. I believe, in this context, that using the term, *"current sound,"* would be a better description rather than calling a sound new. *"God, what is Your current sound? God, what is Your current vibration? What is it that I need to tune into at this very moment, Lord?"*

You have the capability of tuning in to the current sound of God right now! You don't need to wait for someone to *"discover"* a new sound so that you can finally be ushered into a new place in God through it. Go discover His current sound today. Release a new song from within you in response to His current sound today. The true discovery of the *"new sound"* will not be a momentary experience but a continual endeavor as we continually relate to the person and the presence of God.

Helping God Find What He's Seeking

I was made for relationship with God. Ministry is serving others to assist them in their journey with God. When we realize that everything boils down to relationship with the Father God, worship is simply the way we release our half of the relationship to Him. Ministry is first serving God by serving and helping man to join God in relationship, thus releasing their worship to Him as well.

When you take into consideration what God desires from each of His individual children, it's difficult to justify limiting the people of God to certain styles and formats of worship and expression. God desires the unique songs and sounds of each of us, and He has unique songs and sounds to release to us as well.

As a minister, my goal is to see others released into being themselves before the Lord so that He may receive the homemade praises of His children throughout the earth. I'm simply proposing that we all consider what the Father desires. Jesus said the Father is seeking worshippers who will worship Him in spirit and in truth. My desire is to serve God by helping others engage into His presence so that the Father can find what He's seeking.

---

[1] Geoffrey Wainwright/Karen B. Westerfield Tucker, *The Oxford History of Christian Worship* (Oxford University Press, USA), 770.

[2] Ibid., 772-773.

[3] Net Bible. Retrieved November 5, 2009 from http://classic.net.bible.org/strong.php?id=08416

[4] Net Bible. Retrieved November 5, 2009 from http://classic.net.bible.org/strong.php?id=03427

[5] Hennings, Mark R. (2004) Patent Genius. Retrieved October 7, 2011 from http://www.patentgenius.com/patent/7247782.html

Chapter Three
The Potential of God's Presence

When I think of the word potential, one of the first things I think about is sports. I visualize a coach observing a young, raw talent and saying to himself, "*Man, that kid has potential.*" My interests growing up were not in music and the arts, but rather in sports and the great outdoors. I dabbled in team sports in high school, but I could never bring myself to care about sports as much as those guys did. I just wanted to play sports for fun, so that's what I did for the most part. My favorite sport to play was basketball, but I preferred a game of twenty-one over an organized game any day. During my high school days, I began to realize I had a natural ability to jump that went beyond the average person. As a 5'10" junior, I began to be able to dunk a basketball with two hands. If you don't have a clue, for a white boy that is really good! Eventually I was able to do the kinds of dunks you see in dunk contests on TV and on the Internet. I wish I had videotaped myself back then, because those days are over!

In my senior year, I began to think about my potential as a high jumper on the track and field team. The thing was, I had never gone out for track and field in my entire life. I had no idea how well I would do, especially against the competition. As the season drew near, I decided to go for it and I joined the team as a first-year senior. I remember when some of my classmates found out I was joining. One of the guys looked at me and asked if I was joining the team. When I told him that I was, he just laughed at me. So much for the support of my classmates! But I had decided that, no matter what others said, I was going to try this thing. I am glad I didn't let what my classmate said affect me in a negative way. In reality, it made me even more determined to press forward.

I was ready to try this thing!

Press Into the Potential

Potential is latent qualities that may be developed and lead to future success and usefulness.[1] Latent means existing, but not yet made manifest.[2] I knew that I possessed physical abilities that had the potential to lead to success in track and field. I just needed to put myself into a position to utilize these abilities and turn them into success on the field. Potential, in itself, does not mean very much until we decide to utilize that potential. I could have chosen to not join the track and field team. My life would have gone on and I would have been fine. But I did not want to be that person that looked back on what might have been. I wanted to press into the potential to see what would take place.

The team began holding practices only a few weeks before the first track and field meet. I did not have much coaching at all. I was just taking my raw ability and practicing jumping over a bar for a few weeks. Let me mention that I will never attempt to argue with anyone on the quality of my jumping form. I had none. In fact, my jumping form probably looked ugly in accordance with the standards of correct high jumping form. But, I figured, it was not so much about the form as it was about reaching my goals. My first goal was to do the best that I could do. I really had no idea how well I would stack up against the competition. The other major goal I had for the season was to glorify the Lord with the talent that He had given me. I remember telling God that I would glorify Him through the talent He gave me if such an opportunity should ever arise.

Our first track and field meet had arrived and I won the meet, jumping a height of 5'8". For those of you that don't know, the world record for the men's high jump is 8'1/2".

The Potential of God's Presence

Obviously, the height I jumped that day was nowhere near incredible, but it was enough to win my first meet. As the season went along, I began to improve with more training and practice. In reality, for a good part of the season, I was my own competition. Mid-way through the season my next goal became the school record of 6'3", a record that had been in place for over 10 years. We had a home meet coming up, and I remember psyching myself up in the lunchroom where the track and field records were proudly displayed in our tiny high school. I remember just staring up at the board, jumping around the lunchroom yelling, "*SIX-THREE! SIX-THREE!*" I walked down to the field, did my warm ups, and that night I jumped 6'3" and tied the school record.

A few months before that night, I was just a skinny kid with potential. But on that night, I became the official school high jump record-holder. I continued through the season, going undefeated leading up to the sectional track and field meet. Prior to the sectional meet, I had never had any serious competition. But on this night, I looked over the stats on the high jump list and noticed one competitor whose previous best that season was 6'2". I had only jumped higher than that once in competition, and that was when I tied the school record earlier that season. I knew that I would have to jump better at this meet than I ever had in my life if I was going to win the meet.

Without getting too technical, in high jump competition each jumper has three attempts at each height. A record is made of how many failed attempts you have as you progress through the meet. These failed attempts come into play in the case of two or more competitors tying at a certain height. If two jumpers tied at the same height, the competitor with the least amount of attempts over the course of the entire competition would emerge as the winner.

As the meet ensued, it boiled down to me and the other competitor at the height of 6'2". We had both cleared

55

the height, but he had reached the clearing of the height in fewer attempts than me. That meant that I had to jump 6'4" to beat him. When I remember this event, I see it in my mind like it's a movie. I had one attempt left at 6'4". My competitor had already scratched out on all three attempts at the height. It all came down to a final jump. If I missed it, my competitor would take first based on default. My only chance for first place was to clear this final jump. I knelt to the ground on one knee, as was my custom, to pray and ask the Lord for strength. In my mind, I went through all of the training, the practice and the work that I had put into in the season. I remembered the scoffs and laughter of my classmates and the encouragement of my family and friends.

I can remember like it was yesterday as I sailed over the bar. I crashed down onto the landing mat, looked up, and there it was. The bar was still there! I had done it. I had never done it before, and I have never done it since, but on that warm spring night I had cleared 6'4" and won first place in the high jump at the Northern Illinois Sectional Track and Field Meet. In my first and only year of competition, I was heading to the Illinois State High Jump Finals. After the meet the local paper interviewed me. In the interview, I was able to let the entire Northern Illinois region know that I had dedicated my season to glorifying the Lord Jesus Christ. It was He who had gifted me with my talent and ability, and I wanted to give glory and honor back to Him. When the article came out, it had a big picture of me jumping over the bar with a title in large, black print that read, "*Leap of Faith Vaults Heilman Down-State.*" Needless to say, it was a great feeling and one of the most memorable events of my life.

I took you through that season of my life with the intent of exemplifying what can happen when potential is mixed with expectation and action. The potential to become an award-winning athlete was within me as a senior in high school, but I had to make a decision to take the steps necessary to tap into that potential. When I began to understand the potential I had, it created an expectation within me that I could succeed. That expectation led me to take action so that I could realize the expectations that were in me. As I moved forward, the more potential I realized, the more I began to expect and thus the more I achieved.

I believe that this progression translates over into our relationship with God. We first need to realize who God is. Through the Word of God, we need to develop our understanding of His character, His majesty, and His promises. **The measure of one's knowledge of God will determine the measure of one's expectation of God.** In recent years, instead of praying for people to have more faith in God, I've begun to ask God to increase in others their understanding and realization of who He is. In Matthew 17, Jesus said that we only needed faith the size of a mustard seed to move mountains. We don't need big faith; we just need a little faith in a big God. The first step in truly realizing the full potential of God's presence is to continually *"be knowing"* Him. As you begin to realize who He truly is, it will increase your expectations and it will eventually change the way you live your life.

Priority One: Get to Know Who God Is

In Ephesians 1:16–19a, Paul writes, *"I have not stopped giving thanks for you, remembering you in my prayers. I keep asking that the God of our Lord Jesus Christ, the glorious Father, may give you the Spirit of wisdom and revelation, so that you may know him better. I pray that the eyes of your heart may be enlightened in order that you may know the hope to which he has called you, the riches of his glorious inheritance in his holy people, and his incomparably great power for us who believe."*

In this passage, Paul starts by praying for the Ephesians to gain wisdom and revelation for the purpose of getting to know God better. This scripture really gives us insight into how we progress into what God has for us. It starts with our relationship with Him. It starts with knowing Him. God wants us to know Him. God wants to have a relationship with us. He wants to reveal who He is to us.

Paul continues to pray, in this passage of scripture, that the eyes of the Ephesians' hearts would be enlightened for the purposes of knowing the hope that God called them to and His incomparably great power for those who believe. It seems that Paul knew that the Ephesians' understanding of this hope and power would flow out of their understanding of God Himself. If you are going to put your hope in God, you need to know that God is a God in whom you can trust. If you need power to live this life, you need to know that God is a God of immeasurable power and that He wants to empower you daily.

Realize that the key to accessing the full potential of the presence and power of God is a deep knowledge of God. The measure of your expectation in God will only be as great as your knowledge of the promises of the Word of God. I also believe that the depth and width of a person's experience in the presence of God is related to their knowledge of the character and person of God.

Knowledge + Expectation + Action Equals Power

> Mark 5:25–34: *"And a woman was there who had been subject to bleeding for twelve years. She had suffered a great deal under the care of many doctors and had spent all she had, yet instead of getting better she grew worse. When she heard about Jesus, she came up behind him in the crowd and touched his cloak, because*

she thought, 'If I just touch his clothes, I will be healed.' Immediately her bleeding stopped and she felt in her body that she was freed from her suffering. At once Jesus realized that power had gone out from him. He turned around in the crowd and asked, 'Who touched my clothes?' 'You see the people crowding against you,' his disciples answered, 'and yet you can ask, "Who touched me?"' But Jesus kept looking around to see who had done it. Then the woman, knowing what had happened to her, came and fell at his feet and, trembling with fear, told him the whole truth. He said to her, 'Daughter, your faith has healed you. Go in peace and be freed from your suffering.'"

This woman is one of the greatest examples in scripture of someone who knew how to position herself to receive what she needed from the Lord. I want to take you through the progression that she took in order that we may learn from her example.

The first thing that she did was to identify her need. She was in need of physical healing. No doctor had been able to help her for twelve years. She was desperate for an answer to the issue she was dealing with in her life. When we come into the presence of the Lord, we need to identify our needs as well. Hebrews 4:15-16 says, *"For we do not have a high priest (Jesus) who is unable to sympathize with our weaknesses, but we have one who has been tempted in every way, just as we are—yet was without sin. Let us then approach the throne of grace with confidence, so that we may receive mercy and find grace to help us in our time of need."* Jesus came to this earth in order to understand what we, as human beings, go through. I am thankful, when I talk with the Lord and tell him what I am dealing with, that I know He knows what I am talking about. When we approach Jesus, we can rest fully assured that He understands right where we are at and that He is ready to pour His grace out upon us.

The Scripture says that this woman heard about Jesus. In the context of this passage, it is saying that she'd heard that Jesus was near. But, it is also obvious that the reputation of who Jesus was had been previously heard by her. She had heard stories of the man who cleansed the leper, gave sight to the blind and cast demons from the possessed. This woman knew about Jesus the Healer. Her knowledge of who Jesus was created an excitement, anticipation and expectation within her. She knew The Potential of His Presence. She knew that when Jesus was near, healing could take place. It is important that we develop, through the Word of God, our knowledge of who Jesus is. When we know who He is, we will then know what we can expect of Him.

This woman was moved to action based on what she knew about Jesus. The Scripture says that a large crowd was surrounding Jesus, and that this woman had to literally press through the crowd to get to Him. I love the desperation of this woman! She was not content to see Jesus from a distance, hoping that He might notice her. James 2:20 says, *"Faith without works is dead."* Her faith and expectation in Jesus led her to action. It led her to press past her circumstances to touch Jesus. God really wants you to find Him. When I enter into a time of seeking the Lord, I don't HOPE that I will encounter God. I know that I will! I may not encounter the Lord the way I did last time, but I will encounter Him all the same.

When this woman touched the hem of Christ's garment, the Word says that Jesus noticed that power went out from Him. Jesus literally felt the power that was within Him flow out from Him into the woman's body. The interesting thing is that there were actually lots of people touching Jesus at the same time that the woman touched Him. He was in a large crowd and people were bumping up against Him constantly. What was so different about this woman's touch from that of the rest of the crowd? There is a difference between a casual touch and a purposeful touch. There were lots of people casually coming into contact with Jesus that day, but the Word of God does not record anything about them. I believe the example of this woman shows us that we need to be more than casual observers of Jesus Christ. Her expectation literally drew the power of Jesus into her situation. She was a woman of knowledge, expectation and action and her life changed forever because of it.

Wait On the Lord

God is continually teaching me about the calling and anointing upon my life as a prophetic minstrel. I recently had an enlightening experience at a meeting that we held in Houston, TX. While preparing for the meeting, the Lord gave me further insight on how to lead people to the vast places of His presence. One of the things I have been learning as a prophetic minstrel is that people are not always ready to jump right into the spontaneous flow of the Spirit. I've had experiences where I have tried to just flow right into the prophetic, and for the most part, people weren't inclined to jump right in.

The Lord told me to split the meeting into three parts. First, we started with a time of singing some familiar worship songs. Second, I took a brief time to exhort the people how to position themselves in the presence of God and what to expect in His presence. Third, I began to create a musical atmosphere conducive to the prophetic. I began to sing prophetic songs and words of knowledge over the people. The people were very engaged in what the Lord was doing. Afterwards many of the people told me how blessed they were and what the Lord had spoken to them.

Through this and other experiences, I have come to realize that people are generally more used to speaking and singing to God than they are used to listening to God speak and sing to them. In Houston, the Lord told me I needed to encourage the people to wait on Him. Once they were encouraged to do so, and once they realized that the second half of the gathering was set aside for the purpose of waiting on God, encounters began to happen.

This occurrence prompted me to think about how little time is devoted to waiting on the Lord in the midst of worship gatherings. From my observance here in America, people seem to get uncomfortable sometimes in a worship service if you don't keep the songs going. People are not used to musical interludes in the midst of a song, set aside for the purpose of their own personal reflection on God. In the past, I have sometimes received puzzled looks as I have tried to move Sunday morning worship services from people telling to people listening. My goal is to see people encounter God, not a song. I know that God wants to speak to people. But the form in a lot of churches for worship seems to be set up for one-way communication, from man to God. Consider with me that it's time to even out, if you will, the format of our gathering in order to give more time for the purpose of waiting upon and hearing from the Lord.

Realizing Potential Is Just the Beginning

It's one thing to know that something has potential, another to realize what the potential is and entirely another thing to engage into the potential. Just like the woman with the issue of blood, we need to go from thinking there might be something to this Jesus guy to realizing what that *"something"* is and ultimately to pressing in to touch Him.

Ephesians 3:17b–19 says, *"And I pray that you, being rooted and established in love, may have power, together with all the Lord's holy people, to grasp how wide and long and high and deep is the love of Christ, and to know this love that surpasses knowledge that you may be filled to the measure of all the fullness of God."*

Paul prays for the Ephesians that they may grasp the fullness of the love of Christ. Notice that he mentions that this love *"surpasses knowledge."* The love of God surpasses even our minds' ability to grasp its fullness. So why then would Paul pray that the Ephesians would yet grasp it? This understanding is found in a place beyond our minds, a place that we can only engage in with our spirits. There is an unlimited potential in God that goes beyond our finite comprehension. I would never attempt to reveal in this book the endless potential of the presence and person of God. My desire is that we would all be spiritually awakened to a greater understanding and awareness of His character that will accordingly inspire us to pursue the potential of the presence of God.

---

[1] "Potential." Oxford American Dictionary. 2nd ed. 2005.

[2] "Latent." Oxford American Dictionary. 2nd ed. 2005.

Chapter Four
Positioned for God's Presence

I have such a desire to see people more fully engage into the potential of the presence of God. It is so important that we learn how to approach the Lord to position and posture ourselves to encounter Him. We don't want to miss what the Lord's doing because we aren't positioned to connect with Him. This *"missing"* does not just happen in the context of people missing what God is doing. This *"missing"* can also happen in our relationships with each other. Let me give you a few examples.

I remember once when my wife and I went to hear a friend do a stand-up comedy routine. Now let me just tell you that this friend of mine is very funny and so I was looking forward to hearing the routine. Unfortunately, it did not go very well for my friend for a number of reasons. First of all, the room was so large that is was hard to get people's attention. Atmosphere has a lot to do with how people are engaged. Second, there was a lot of distraction going on in the room, which made it hard for people to concentrate on just him. Third, and I think the biggest issue, was that these people did not come just to hear a comedy routine. It was more of a variety night, so his comedy act was just one part of the evening. It proves that people receive what they expect. If they are not expecting something, they are not open to receive it and they usually won't. The fact that people were not laughing had nothing to do with the fact that my friend was not hilarious. It had a lot more to do with the fact that the people were not focused, open and expecting to laugh.

Another example comes from something that my wife recently encountered. As a professional dancer, she has performed countless times in front of various crowds. Recently she and some other dancers ministered through dance in front of a large group of Christian leaders. Recounting the dance, my wife pointed out the fact that only a few people seemed to really be ministered to. Previously, they had done this dance in other venues and hundreds of people across the nation had been impacted by their ministry of movement. So why weren't these people? Again, I believe it was because the people there did not posture themselves to receive from the Spirit of God through the ministry of the dancers.

Am I Missing Something?

The presence of God is often near without us realizing it. I remember I was waiting to board a plane at the DFW airport to minister somewhere. I was sitting in the terminal reading the paper when, all of a sudden, a little bird flew right next to my head. I freaked out for a second, and then I made sure that nobody noticed. The last thing I expect when sitting in the airport is for a bird to fly by my face. After I laughed to myself, I traded in reading the paper for watching the bird. It began flying all over the place, circling around people's heads. Some noticed, but I laughed at how many people were oblivious to the fact that a bird was flying a few feet from their heads in the airport, yet they had no clue. How many times have you or I missed an opportunity to connect to the presence of God? I can tell you there are many times I have gazed at a sunset in the West Texas sky and praised God for the beauty of His creation. I can also guarantee that countless others under the same sky gave not one thought to the Creator or His creation. God is giving us plenty of opportunities to encounter Him and He's looking for those that will take the time to position themselves to connect with Him.

Human Lightning Streamers

I was in Tampa Bay, FL, ministering for a weekend worship gathering. I had been to Tampa numerous times before, but I learned something new on this trip about the Tampa area. Tampa Bay is known as the Lightning Capital of North America. More lightning strikes occur here than in any other area of the continent. The word *"Tampa"* means *"sticks of fire"* in the language of the Calusa, a Native American tribe that once lived in the region.[1]

One night the pastor and I were driving toward the city and one after another, bolts of lightning began to strike throughout the clouds. I have always been fascinated with weather, and would probably be a storm chaser if I were not in the ministry. When I was in Florida gazing at all that lightning, I remembered a picture I had seen online of what is called a lightning streamer. The photo was of a tree being struck by lightning, but off to the side of the tree you can see a small line of light sticking up on another part of the tree. I later learned that this is a lightning streamer. A lightning streamer is a positive charge that sticks up from any source on the ground. The lightning streamer often will determine that path of cloud-to-ground lightning. The streamer actually presents itself to the sky as a source of connection. God really began to speak to me through this about our responsibility to position ourselves before the Lord. We are to be like these lightning streamers. The potential to connect with heaven is available; we just need to be pro-active and present ourselves before the Lord. God is just looking to connect with those that will make themselves available to Him.

Sacrifice Equals Fire

I love the story of the dedication of the Temple of Solomon. In 2 Chronicles 7:1 it reads, *"Now when Solomon had made an end of praying, the fire came down from heaven, and consumed the burnt offering and the sacrifices; and the glory of the LORD filled the house."* (KJV) There is something about a sacrifice that moves God to manifest something from Heaven into the natural realm. Solomon put a sacrifice upon the altar and the Lord responded with fire. A connection was made.

In Romans 12, Paul tells us to present our bodies unto the Lord as living sacrifices. In Hebrews 13, we are instructed to give God a sacrifice of praise. We no longer give sacrifices of bulls and sheep unto the Lord, but sacrifices that come directly from us ourselves. It is clear that God responds to our sacrifices. But in order to connect with God, we need to be intentional and purposeful. We need to offer up our sacrifices of praise with an expectation that when we do, we will encounter the fire of His presence.

Are You HD Ready?

My wife and I purchased our first High Definition (HD) ready wide-screen television and we are really enjoying it now. I say *"now"* because the first time I set it up, I was not enjoying it at all. It did not look anything like what it looked like in the store when I hooked it up to my cable box to watch TV. I later realized, through my extensive research, that the cord I was using to connect the cable box to the TV was the worst possible cord I could have used. The low quality of the cord resulted in a terrible transmission of the picture, and thus caused my dissatisfaction on that initial day. The next day, I went out and bought some new cords and hooked them

The Potential of God's Presence

up. The picture looked so much better than it had the day before, and needless to say, I was a lot happier.

When the cable company announced they were going to broadcast all of their HD channels free for one week, I had not yet decided on whether or not I wanted to pay for the extra HD service. I was glad to be able to try out the channels to see if there would be much difference. I will be honest and say that I did not really think there would be much difference. I was wrong. I was amazed at how much clearer the picture was on the HD channels. After I watched a few shows in HD, I really began to notice just how much of a difference there was between High Definition and the Standard Definition of the regular channels. You might say that my viewing of the High Definition channels ruined me for the Standard.

I was glad that I had just gotten the HD-ready TV so that I could see what HD channels looked like. If I'd still had my good old twenty-seven inch box TV set up during free HD week, it would not have mattered because my old TV would not have been able to receive the High-Definition signal. The Lord really began to speak to me through all of this recently. I am so glad I can justify the purchase of my new TV because I now realize it was the Lord's will for me to buy it so that He could share the following deep revelation with me.

I believe that the Lord desires every one of us to go into the great depths of His presence. The Word of God says in Psalm 42:7, *"Deep calls to deep in the roar of your waterfalls; all your waves and breakers have swept over me."* I believe there are vast realms of His presence that He is calling us to enter into. We just have to position ourselves correctly to receive this call and respond to it from the depths of ourselves. The Word does not say, *"Deep calls to surface."* It says, *"Deep calls to deep."*

I believe that a reason why people are not going to broader and expanded places in God's presence is because they have become accustomed to and content with a certain standard of worship experience. An example of one of these standards is the simple singing of songs in church. It is the process of getting three fast songs and two slow songs together and singing them back to back, making sure there is no, what some call "*dead time*", in between. There is very often no time given in the midst this standard worship gathering to seek the Lord a personal way. The worship service had been pre-planned and defined by the pastor and/or worship leader. This type of worship service is usually focused much more on what we are going to tell God than it is on taking time to hear what He might have to say back. It is one-way communication.

This format of worship service is what you will generally find in many Western modern-day Sunday morning church gatherings. HEAR ME: These meetings are not void of God's presence. Understand that I am not trying to bring any negativity to the way that churches are choosing to format worship services today. God is present and moving in people's lives in those meetings. But I do believe that God is calling out in this hour for the church to expand its view of the worship experience! God wants us to expand our standard of what it means to meet with Him. I believe it is true that you will get what you expect. Whatever standard you set, you will reach.

I want to refer back to my TV analogy here. If I had still had my old standard definition TV set plugged into my cable box during free HD week, it would not have mattered how much I would have loved to see HD on my old TV set. It could not have happened because the **reception standard** on my old TV was too low to be able to receive the HD signal. That cable box could be sending HD signals all day long, but it would not matter on that old set because it was not equipped to receive such a high signal level. The standard of "*The Receiver*" was not high enough for the higher standard of HD signal.

We need to posture ourselves for what the Lord wants to release to us. We need to stop acting like old standard TVs. God is trying to get us to understand that He created us to receive so much more than what we've realized. He is crying out from His deep to the depths of who we are. He wants to pour it out to us, but we need to position ourselves to receive it. It's time for us to upgrade our expectations. We cannot stand upon the standard of yesterday and expect to go into the depths of today!

We need to thank God for where we have been. I am thankful for the ways I have connected with Him in the past. But I don't want to stop there. I want to explore into the depths of the fullness of who He is, and I know I won't be able to do that when I have parameters already defined for me ahead of time. If I am going to discover the deep of God, I am going to need the space, the time and the freedom to be able to explore His presence.

First-Hand Revelation

Since my initial journey to the beautiful land of Hawaii on my honeymoon, I have been to the islands for a total of six times as of this writing. It is true that once you go to Hawaii, it somehow calls you back time and time again. My wife and I have fallen in love with Hawaii, the people and their culture. Of course, like anyone else that travels, we take pictures and videos of our journeys in order to help us remember the great things we saw and experienced.

Some of you, as I describe the amazing times I have had in this tropical paradise, may already be saying to yourself, "*Okay, okay enough already,*" especially if you have never been there before.

When I am talking about Hawaii when I preach, I ask people how excited they would be if I offered to show them a slide presentation of all of my photos of my vacations. Nobody gets excited at this proposal. The look on their faces seems to say; *"Now why would I want to look at all of your pictures?"* I go on to ask how many of them would like it if I offered them two round-trip tickets to go to Hawaii themselves. Even at the mention of this, without it even being a remote possibility, people start smiling and getting excited. People start laughing and raising their hands, some saying, *"Oh me, me!"* Of course I have no tickets for them, but the point is made by the people themselves, that they would much rather go to Hawaii than see my pictures of Hawaii. The people would much rather experience the Islands firsthand than look through photos of my experience. I go on to ask, *"Then why are we content to settle for the second-hand revelation of others when it comes to discovering the Lord?"*

If I could sum it up clearly, second-hand is good but first-hand is better. There is a place for the second-hand revelation. As I have stated, it should not be thrown out nor should it be our ultimate goal. Rather, it should create inspiration and zeal within us to experience what others have experienced, but in our own personal way.

One of Music's Greatest Purposes Is for Recreation

I believe that people usually end up receiving what they anticipate or expect. If you expect nothing you will probably end up with nothing. If somebody expects to be entertained, they will probably be entertained. One of the things that the Lord desires to do in atmospheres of music created by minstrels is to bring refreshing, rejuvenation and re-creation. Because our society is so entertainment-based, it's important that we shift out of our entertainment mentalities in order to approach God in these musical atmospheres with the proper expectations. I can fully intend to create an atmosphere for someone to enter into the re-creative presence of God, but if they have not prepared their expectations toward this, they will possibly miss what the Lord wants to do. Entertainment is a form of maintenance and God is not a maintainer but a renewer and re-creator.

The increasing reality of the global culture is that we are an entertainment-based society. I believe that many are increasingly engaging in various venues of entertainment as a form of escapism from their particular realities. Our entertainers are becoming the maintainers of this escape from reality. The problem is that entertainment can never truly satisfy the desire each of us has for peace, joy and contentment. Only the presence of God can truly do this.

As human beings, we are not meant to escape from reality, but rather to engage in the greater reality of the power and presence of God and His Kingdom. Entertainment can oftentimes give us a false sense of refreshing, but as soon as the entertainment is over, this feeling goes with it. This causes people to continually seek after entertainment to maintain a false sense of peace, joy or renewal.

The origin of the word entertain comes from the French word entretenir, based on Latin inter 'among' + tenere 'to hold.' It means to maintain in a certain condition.[2] When you look deeper into what it means to entertain, you find that an entertainer is one who maintains or provides others maintenance with their gift of entertainment.

Something that I have noticed about entertainment is that the pleasures of entertainment are so fleeting. There have been times when my wife and I have planned months in advance to see a show. We marked it on our schedule and looked forward to it with anticipation. One Christmas season, my wife and I went to an orchestra performance in Dallas. It was a great show, but like all forms of entertainment, it came to an end. I felt very warm and nostalgic during the performance, but those feelings were short lived as we ran out into the cold night air towards our car for the drive home.

The musicians played for us, the singers sang for us and we were entertained. We expected to be entertained and so we were. We expected to sit in a beautiful theatre and have others bring warm, nostalgic feelings and memories to us through the singing and playing of timeless Christmas classics. We didn't have to do anything but sit, relax and enjoy. That is the point of entertainment. You pay someone to perform and make you happy so you can enjoy escaping the real world for a sliver of time. The sad part is, reality is waiting for you at the exit door. Monday morning calls from a distance, and you try to ignore its voice for as long as you can through each weekend.

Many musicians throughout history and up to our present day have often used their gifts given by God for entertainment rather than re-creation. David was a minstrel that operated in a spirit of re-creation. Through David's music, Saul was re-created and tuned into the vibe of God. Entertainers tune people into the vibe of their charismatic personalities. This vibe ceases to be with us once we leave that entertainer's presence.

Johann Sebastian Bach once said, *"Music's only purpose should be for the glory of God and the recreation of the human spirit."*[3] Bach, highly regarded as one of the world's all-time greatest composers, knew something about music that many people have forgotten. Not only is music's purpose for the glorification of God, but also for the re-creation of the human spirit. Music was given to us by God as a re-creative tool.

Recreation is defined as mental or spiritual consolation. It derives from the French word recreare, to renew or create again.[4] It's activity that refreshes and re-creates, activity that renews your health and spirits by enjoyment and relaxation.

You Are a Participant in Your Own Re-creation

A major difference I noticed between entertainment and re-creation is that entertainment requires no participation on behalf of the entertained, whereas the ones who are re-created are required to actively become a part of their own re-creation. A phrase that has become popular within some church circles is "*soaking*." There are people that like to get in a room and lie on the floor as musicians play and sing over them. Soaking can take on a form of entertainment when we begin to rely upon the music or musician to maintain our peace and rest instead of the presence of the Lord. Yes, I just said that, but hear me out. I was leading a night of Rejuvenation and people started showing up with their pillows and sleeping bags and proceeded to camp out on the floor. I thought it was cool, but looking back on it, I wonder how many of those campers left with what God had for them that night. Music, in itself, has the power to relax us and induce peace and joy in our lives. The problem is, when the music stops, so does the peace and joy. That is why it is important, in the midst of the atmosphere, to enter into the presence of Jesus to receive what He has for you. When you get what God has for you, that which He gives will be that which sustains you. The music is not what sustains us; it is what assists us to come into the presence of The Sustainer. Sometimes it's not as much an issue of the intent of the musician, rather it's the expectation of the person lying on the floor with his/her sleeping bag. Re-creation requires that we enter into the presence of the Lord to hear what He is saying in order that we may move with His word. I've personally known people that have gone to these "*soaking meetings*" for years and they are still dealing with issues in their lives in the same way they were years ago. It's possible that they have made these soaking times a form of escapism instead of a place in which they can get a download from God that will transform them.

Isaiah 40:31 says, *"But they that wait upon the Lord shall renew their strength."* (KJV) It's important, in the context of this verse, to understand the concept of what God means by waiting. The waiting that is mentioned here is an active waiting. Instead of visualizing the eagle sitting around in its nest waiting, visualize the eagle on the edge of its nest waiting for the winds. I believe that God desires us to be a people that wait with anticipation, people that are proactive in searching for what He is doing and speaking in our midst.

The Lens of Entertainment

One thing that I have talked to my wife about is the frustration that artists face when those that are the recipients of their art form totally miss what they tried to convey. She may release an anointed dance under the unction of the Holy Spirit in order to release a revelation from God that she is receiving in the moment. Then, after the meeting, someone might come up to her and say, *"That was a really neat dance."* You can tell that they missed what God was trying to convey because they looked at her dance through the lens of entertainment.

As recipients of the art of the minstrels, whether the minstrels are dancers, musicians or artists, people need to remove the lens of entertainment to perceive and receive what God is trying to convey through them. I tell people that they need to search for the meaning of the art rather than just receive it at face value, as entertainment. I can actually tell what my wife is dancing about when I watch her and receive from the Lord that which she is trying to convey through her art form. I can also hear things in music that God is revealing when I hear an anointed minstrel play on his/her instrument. What can happen is that people have become so culturally accustomed to just sitting back to be entertained that they don't realize that it's necessary to search for what God is trying to say through prophetic sound, movement or art.

Bread & Circuses

"The people who once upon a time handed out military command, high civil office, legions — everything, now restrains itself and anxiously hopes for just two things: bread and circuses."[5]

The previous is a quote from Juvenal, a Roman poet active in the late 1st and 2nd century AD. He lived in the times of the great Roman stadiums, chariot races and the Gladiators. Juvenal here makes reference to the Roman practice of providing free wheat to some poor Romans as well as costly circus games and other forms of entertainment. There is no question that the Roman governmental system of that day used various forms of entertainment to distract the people from the real issues the day. Entertainment was used to channel the common people's energy into these activities so that they would stay disengaged from the issues of society.

In his quote, Juvenal makes it clear that people were no longer moving in their fullest potential as a people because they were settling for food and games. The people no longer had vision or drive because these forces within them were now displaced into the vein of entertainment. He goes as far to say that the people restrained themselves from moving upon their passions as they settled for what the governing powers were feeding them.

While entertainment can be enjoyable in moderation, it is clear that when it becomes a part of one's lifestyle, entertainment can literally neutralize an individual from living out their potential. Entertainment can take leaders and make them into followers. It can potentially take creative thinkers and reform their thoughts into the formula of society.

What Happened to Our Imaginations?

Imagination can be defined as the action of forming ideas, images or concepts of external objects not present to the senses. Often, imagination is associated with children and their ability to create an imaginary friend or world. My wife told me that when she was a young child she used to look closely into the mirror and imagine someone from another world staring back at her from the other side. Although the imagination is often used in the realm of childhood fantasy, the imagination also has its place in everyday, adult reality.

My Grandpa used to work for a machine shop before he retired. I used to love to hang out with him and just let him tell me stories. He once told me some stories about his job. Oftentimes, the machines in the shop where he worked would break down. When this happened, my Grandpa told me he would go back to the locker room, lie down on a bench and just quiet himself. He said he would imagine the machine and all of its parts working correctly. As he began to do this, he would begin to see how the machine operated when it was functioning correctly. He would then get back up, go out to the machine and fix it immediately. He told me that *"the man upstairs"* would always show him how to fix it. At the time, it was just a cool story. Now, I realize that my Grandpa was partnering his God-given imagination with the Holy Spirit. He would go into the locker room, position himself before the Lord and listen for the still small voice of instruction from the One who knows all things. This is a prime example of how someone can utilize their imagination in the presence of the Lord to receive answers from the Father for living everyday life.

The imagination acts like a translator that transforms information from the spirit realm into concepts that our minds can understand. The power of the imagination lies in its ability to create scenarios and images within the mind.

Have you ever stopped to think that everything that has ever been invented was once only a visual image within an inventor's mind? The invention began in the imagination of the inventor. Even God Himself thought of us before we physically existed. Jeremiah 1:5 says, *"Before I formed you in your mother's womb I knew you...."* Before we were created, God had us in His imagination. He had plans for us before we were created and eventually brought forth those plans into the natural realm.

I believe that in order to live out God's fullest potential for each of our lives; we must have our imaginations in good working order. The imagination is given to us by God in order that we might translate the instructions of God into reality in our lives. If our imaginations are weak, we are going to miss some of the things that God desires to reveal to us. How, then, do our imaginations become weakened? Just like a muscle in the physical body, if the imagination is not used, it will weaken and wither. The greatest reason why our imaginations grow weak is simply due to the fact that we are not using them.

The Lord revealed to me that the current entertainment culture holds the potential to rob a generation of their imagination. Just one generation ago, kids were playing games of imagination and make-believe. Now kids don't have to imagine anymore. This generation has so much visual stimulation being presented to it that they don't need an imagination anymore. They could justifiably argue, *"Why should I need to imagine, I can just turn on my TV, computer or videogame system and escape into a virtual world with no effort on my part whatsoever."* An entertaining, visual society does much in leading to lethargy in a generation.

I no doubt may be rubbing some the wrong way with such statements, especially the gamers out there. But consider why the statistics of my generation regarding church attendance exist. It's estimated that 80% of those currently

18-30 have had significant church experience during high school. That means they consistently attended church or a Bible study or a youth group for two months or longer. Of that 80%, only 20% of them have stayed connected.[6] Obviously there is more than one reason why these statistics are true. But I believe a major reason that these statistics exist is due to the fact that our generation does not know how to use their imaginations anymore. They don't know how to connect to the Lord spirit to Spirit. If they no longer need to imagine in a virtual, entertainment culture then why should we expect them to come into church and imagine that there is a God, Whom they can't see, that loves them and has a plan for their lives?

They can't fully because the Word of God tells us that we can't fully see what God has for us with our natural senses. I Corinthians 2:9–10 says, *"What no eye has seen, what no ear has heard, what no mind has conceived — the things God has prepared for those who love him — these are the things God has revealed to us by his Spirit. The Spirit searches all things, even the deep things of God."* We need our imaginations to be strong, if only to be able to see beyond the natural circumstances of our lives and into the supernatural plans that God has for us.

We need to begin asking God to heal the imaginations of a generation! We also need to begin creating atmospheres in which their imaginations can be strengthened. What is happening in our churches is that we have recognized that our culture is very visual and entertainment-based. Rather than create environments that are conducive to helping others grow in encountering the Lord through their spirits, is it possible that we're simply giving them a sanctified version of what they have been getting in their entertainment culture? If we try to present everything to them, we could potentially be removing opportunity to develop life in the spirit away from them.

Let's Get Practical

I have been in worship services where the leader would energetically exhort the people to praise and worship God. I have done the same thing myself. Some would go as far as to say that that is the worshipper leader's job. I would agree to a certain extent. But each of us should desire to grow past the point of needing others to motivate us towards worshipping the Creator of the Universe. Our goal as leaders in the body of Christ is to essentially teach ourselves out of our jobs. By this I am saying that, although we may have to begin by exhorting people to worship the Lord, the goal is to teach people how to go straight after Him. Growing up in church, I rarely heard much teaching on Sunday mornings about how to actually and practically enter into worship. I've found that it's a rare thing to hear teaching on worship in church. And when it is taught, it is often taught regarding such topics as "*What Is Worship?*" or "*The Seven Words for Praise.*" The fact is, teaching on what worship is will not be enough. We need to begin to teach people specifically and practically how to enter into the presence of the Lord. We need to begin to teach people how to spiritually focus on the Lord and how to position themselves to both sing their songs unto the Lord and listen to the songs that He is singing over them.

In our meetings I have begun to release what I call "*primers*" or small teachings related to worship and listening. What I have experienced is that people will enter into what they are prepared for. When people know what is going on and what to do in the midst of what is happening, they will ultimately enjoy a fuller experience. Releasing these short teachings assists people to understand how to prepare their hearts for what is about to take place. It makes such a difference in how people are able to enter in to where the Lord is leading. Eventually, this will begin to happen more naturally, especially when you lead the same people over a period of time as in the context of a local church.

At a church I formerly served as *Worshipper Pastor*, I taught the people how to enter into times of waiting on the Lord. As a result, they began to release more spontaneous praise and they were no longer leery of extended times of instrumental music in the midst of a worship time. I did not just hope that they would get it. I took time to teach, exhort and share on practical principles that helped them enter more fully into these expressions.

I am thankful that my former pastor allowed me to teach on worship from the pulpit on Sunday mornings. I think it is vital that we do so in our churches. We can't worship fifty-two Sundays a year, never teach on worship once and then expect everyone in the church to just *"get it"* and enter into the fullness of the praise and worship experience. When we don't teach practical things regarding praise, worship and listening, we end up with a church that contains varying degrees of understanding of worship. Teaching on it brings the people together. They begin to understand why things are done the way they are. They begin to learn that instrumental interludes in the service are not meant as a cue for them to check out, but as a time for them to create their own expressions of praise to the Father. They begin to learn that periods of silence are for the discovery of the person and power of God, not for wondering where they will go to lunch after service. Recently I was talking to a good friend who said that it's easy to be busy, but it's hard to wait in the silence. I totally agree with him. But it's in the place of silence where we will discover the very heart of the Father. In the stillness we will find the direction, strategy and wisdom we need to live our lives. In the quiet we will find healing and refreshing for our souls and bodies.

What to Expect at a Rejuvenation Gathering

I've compiled the following principles as a primer for our Rejuvenation Gatherings. I like the word primer, because a primer is meant to prepare. A primer is not meant to be the goal. These principles prime people and prepare them for something, and that something is encountering the person and presence of God.

I remember mowing the lawn as a kid and pressing the primer button on the lawn mower before I started it. When I pressed that primer button, it was saying to the lawn mower, "*Get Ready.*"

Issues sometimes arise during worship when the band stops playing, the leader stops exhorting and the words disappear from the screen. The people can get lost, disoriented and uncomfortable. Would you agree with me that this needs to change? We all need to develop an understanding of how to seek the Lord in the stillness and silence. These times of pausing should not be times of disorientation, confusion and discomfort. They should be times of direction, revelation and peace. Instead of avoiding the issue by filling in every second with activity in our services, we need to begin to teach people how to interact with the Lord in the neutral environments created by the minstrels of the Lord.

So let me share these principles with you now. They are meant to be more than teachings to be placed on the shelves of your mind. They are meant to lead you into a lifestyle of active, participatory waiting as you come before the Lord.

Relationship & Encounter
We all need time to encounter the presence of the Lord to deepen our understanding of who He is and to develop our relationship with Him. Consider the man who "*meditates upon the Lord day and night*" from Psalm 1:2–3. "*He is like a*

tree planted by streams of living water which yields its fruit in season and whose leaf does not wither. Whatever he does prospers." The minstrel is more than a song leader. The minstrel is anointed to create musical atmospheres conducive to others being able to engage in personal revelation of the character and person of the Lord.

Personal Evaluation & Realignment
The business of life can often leave us off-track if we are not taking time to consistently re-evaluate where we are. Galatians 5:25 says, *"Since we live by the spirit, let us stay in step with the spirit."* Consistent personal evaluation is important to avoid the pitfalls of life in family, business and ministry. The minstrel is anointed to create atmospheres where others can effectively *"present their requests unto God"* (Philippians 4:6). It is a time to lay your requests, questions, and concerns before the feet of Jesus in order to keep in alignment with His purpose and plan for your life.

Restoration & Refreshing
Jesus is the One who restores and refreshes. Music is a neutral tool that can be used for positive or negative purposes. Consider the following translation of Psalm 23:1–3: *"I want for nothing, for Adonai is my shepherd: it is God who lets me lie down in pastures of grass and who leads me to calm waters to restore my spirit, who walks me in level pastures as befits a shepherd of sound reputation."* [7] The minstrel creates musical venues in which others can encounter THE Refresher and THE Restorer. David, in 1 Samuel 16, was anointed to play the harp, which brought Saul refreshing. The music and the minstrel can persuade others toward seeking the Lord through their skill and anointing, but it is the Lord who brings restoration and refreshing.

Revelation & Guidance

"When the harpist (minstrel) was playing, the hand of the Lord came upon Elisha and he said (prophesied)..." (2 Kings 3:15). This Scripture is a prime example of what can happen in the context of a musical environment created by the Holy Spirit-inspired minstrel. It is said that Elisha *"called"* for the harpist to play. Elisha knew that the atmosphere created by the music would bring him into prophetic revelation which led to his declaration in 2 Kings 3:16–19. In the context of everyday life, we need the Word of the Lord to be a *"lamp unto our feet, and a light unto our pathway"* (Psalm 119:105). The prophetic word or the word from the Lord, *Dabar*, means to *"get behind and drive forward to completion."* In essence, the atmosphere created by the prophetic minstrel allows God's people to come into His presence to receive a *"guiding word that will drive them into the completion of their destiny in God."*

Healing Soul & Body

Again we emphasize that it is the Lord who heals and brings healing, both physically and emotionally. We believe that the Lord heals through our prayers and the laying on of hands (James 5:14). Upon studying the life of Jesus as Healer, we see many references by which He laid hands upon others and they were healed. We also find references by which people would touch Him and be healed. *"And the whole multitude sought to touch Him, for there went virtue out of Him, and He healed them all"* (Luke 6:19). This virtue speaks of the *"dunamas"* power of God to bring healing. We believe that we can still *"touch"* Jesus in the context of worship and seeking after Him with all our hearts. *"You will seek me and find me when you seek me with all of your hearts"* (Jeremiah 29:13). In the context of music ministry, we have seen, and believe we will continue to see, people healed both emotionally and physically in the presence of the Lord.

Let's Stay Engaged

To engage is to move into position as to come into operation.[8] Engaging into position will eventually lead you to engaging into the function of your purpose and calling in life. Out of the place of engagement with the presence of God will flow the strategies for the walking out of your destiny in God. Engaging in God's presence will cause you to walk in His will.

One of my favorite Scriptures in the context of relationship with God is Genesis 5:24 which reads, *"And Enoch walked with God: and he was not; for God took him."* The Hebrew word for walk in this scripture is Halak. Halak can literally be translated to mean, *"to walk in another's footsteps."*[9] Many of us have followed the footprints of someone in the sand while at the beach. This is the picture of how Enoch walked with God; he literally followed the Lord step by step. A relationship like this requires that we not only speak to the Lord, but listen to Him as well. There will need to be times where we silence ourselves long enough to perceive the next step that He has for us.

Our relationship with God needs to be balanced in the area of communication. In the current pace of society, people often do not take the time to get away to re-focus on what the Lord is saying. This can often leave us confused and frustrated in our life's journey. We need to consistently take time to position and posture ourselves before the Lord in order to engage into His presence so that we may hear what the Spirit of the Lord is saying.

[1] Wikipedia. Retrieved October 7, 2011 from http://en.wikipedia.org/wiki/History_of_Tampa,_Florida

[2] "Entertain." Oxford American Dictionary. 2nd ed. 2005.

[3] John Michael Talbot, *The Lessons of St. Francis* (Penguin, 1998), 97.

[4] "Recreate." Oxford American Dictionary. 2nd ed. 2005.

[5] Wikipedia. Bread and Circuses. Retrieved October 7, 2011 from http://en.wikipedia.org/wiki/Bread_and_circuses

[6] George Barna, *Revolution* (Barna Books/Tyndale House Publishers 2005), 31-32.

[7] Martin Samuel Cohen, *Our Haven and Our Strength: The Book of Psalms* (Aviv Press 2004), Psalm 23.

[8] "Engage." Oxford American Dictionary. 2nd ed. 2005.

[9] Net Bible. Retrieved November 5, 2009 from http://classic.net.bible.org/strong.php?id=01980

Chapter Five
The Sound of God's Presence

"I take advantage of scientific information that helps to qualify the reality of God."[1] Ray Hughes

I have found that the understanding of scientific principles have further helped me to position myself to engage into the presence of God. I believe, as it pertains to music, it is helpful to know how sound and music "*work.*" Many scientists have actually purposefully set out to disprove the existence of God with their studies and experiments. Many times, they have actually been won over to the truth of the existence of God as they have looked into creation and admitted that, "*Only a creator could have done that.*"

Scientific revelations of sound and music should not be reserved only for musicians. It is helpful for everyone to understand such things because greater understanding and knowledge will actually release us into greater depths of wisdom, which is the actual practice of knowledge. Possessing the knowledge and understanding of how to sense what is going on in the spiritual atmosphere will help people engage in the presence of God. As we learn more about God, music and sound, the more we will become activated in the pursuit and finding of His presence in our lives through silence, sound and music.

God Is Light – God Is Sound

1 John 1:5: "*This is the message we have heard from him and declare to you: God is light; in him there is no darkness at all.*"

We can all read 1 John 1:5 and agree that God is light. Although I have not found any Scriptures that blatantly say, "*God is sound,*" if you understand a little science, you will realize that God is light and sound and all at the same time!

Sound is a traveling wave, which is an oscillation of pressure transmitted through a medium of solid, plasma, liquid or gas. The measurement of distance between the peaks of the sound wave is referred to as the frequency. As I like to put it, the frequency is how often or how frequent the peaks of the sound's waves occur. The higher a frequency, the more often the peaks occur. The unit of measurement between the frequencies of sound waves is called a hertz. Hertz is defined as the number of complete cycles per second.

As humans we have the capability of physically hearing roughly in the range of between 20 and 20,000 hertz. On the other hand, red light has a wavelength of about 700 nanometers and relatively has a frequency of almost 429 terahertz, or 429 trillion oscillations or cycles per second. The range of light visible by humans is roughly between 400 and 750 terahertz. As you can see, light has a much higher level of frequency than sound does. On the infinite scale of frequency, these are the small windows of what is able to be picked up by the human senses of hearing and sight. But what about the rest? Is there more to God than meets the eye? Is there more to God than meets our ear? Are there vibrations and frequencies of God than can only be perceived in our spirits, and if so, are we missing vast amounts of revelation available in these realms because we have only been attempting to perceive God with only our natural perceptions?

We believe that there is a supernatural realm. The only reason the term supernatural exists is because of the existence of our limited, natural realm. The supernatural realm is simply all that supersedes the natural realm that we understand and perceive with our physical senses. So, what a natural man deems supernatural, God deems as simply the rest of what WE can't perceive with eyes and ears. There is no supernatural as far as God is concerned. That's why the Word of God says that faith is the substance of things unseen (Hebrews 11:1). There is a realm and substance that exists that we can't sense in the natural. That is why God gave us a spirit so that we could tap into the Spirit of God. Once we learn how to worship and seek and find God in the spirit, whole new vast realms of supernatural revelation open up to us. That is when you start to live a life that supersedes the natural. **It's not that we leave the natural; it's that we add to it.** Again, the supernatural only exists to one who is confined to a limited spectrum. So if God is light and God is sound, God is also all the rest that we can't see and hear with our natural abilities. But God said that He desires to take us to realms in the Spirit that go beyond what our natural senses perceive.

People can't even describe what the inner knowing is because it goes beyond words of description. It's just a knowing that you know. It's the ability that God gave our spirits to rest in that which He has spoken and is continually speaking. Paul prayed for the Philippians that they would possess the peace of God which transcends all understanding (Philippians 4:7). Paul was saying that there is a place of rest that is available in God that is greater that any doubt, worry or fear. Entering this realm of peace requires that we allow God to take us to places beyond our mind, will and emotions.

He Has Given Us the Spirit Which Is of God

1 Corinthians 2:12: *"Now we have received, not the spirit of the world, but the spirit which is of God; that we might know the things that are freely given to us of God."* (KJV)

Throughout First Corinthians Chapter 2, Paul tells the Corinthians that there are things to be received from God that are not within the scope of their finite ears, eyes and mind. He gave us a sprit to enable us to commune with the Holy Spirit, which is of God so that we can know in our spirits the things He has freely given us. What are we possibly missing out on when we are not in tune with His Spirit to hear what He is speaking to us? God told us that we are not going to get it all in the natural. We need to supersede the natural because God's Kingdom and revelation go beyond these natural realms of revelation. That is why the Word of God describes the Holy Spirit as a teacher. The Holy Spirit desires to share insight with your spirit that you can't pick up with your own understanding.

Sound Is Communication

Now that we have looked into some basic principles of light and sound, we realize that sound and light are actually of related substance located at different levels of frequency on the infinite scale of wavelengths. We realized that, through science, we can say with certainty that if God is light, God is also sound.

God is sound and He communicates with sound. This fact enables us to use music as a tool to translate the very heart of God to others. God speaks to us Spirit to spirit, but we communicate to others through touch, sound and sight. How can we take what God has placed in our spirits and reveal it to others? Through movement, vocalization, music and demonstration through the arts God has given us tools to communicate the essence of who He is and what is on His heart. This is what prophetic music and art and dance are, the translation of the very nature and heartbeat of God into a format that people can sense with their natural perceptions.

There are ways to perceive God with our natural senses, but this is only a sliver of the potential of what we can sense. The full spectrum of God is available to us. We can tap into it. We can tune into it. We can run into the shelter of the realities of God and His Kingdom. God wants to take us into supernatural spirit realms in which we can perceive more than what our minds can conceive.

Music can be used to transmit the heart of God into our senses. Prophetic music is translation. While researching I was amazed to realize that the frequencies that radio stations transmit are not the frequencies that we pick up on our radios and ultimately hear. Radio stations transmit what is known as *Radio Light*. These frequencies of transmission are located much higher on the spectrum than the actual radio waves that we eventually hear. The radio receiver actually acts as a translator between these two frequencies. The receiver's purpose is to pick up the high levels of frequency from the station and then transform them into the frequency format that our ears can hear.

Minstrels do the same thing when they release musical vibrations that are re-presentations of what they are sensing from the Spirit of God. Because of the limitations of our abilities to release the spiritual, some things will inevitably be *"lost in translation."* That is why I am such an advocate for first-hand revelation because this revelation comes direct from the *"station,"* so to speak.

God is sound, therefore sound carries within it a potential for the revelation of God's very nature if we will first, as musicians, deliberately use it for this purpose and, secondly, that those that hear it would search the music and find God within it. I have come to realize that different instruments have been anointed to reveal specific realms of God's nature because those notes at those specific frequencies literally represent God. For example, the violin is an instrument that releases high notes across high frequencies. These specific frequencies hold within them the potential to release divine revelation of the very nature of God. Typically when I hear the violin I am taken to places of soothing peace. God is peace, God is sound and the frequencies of God that represent peace are found in instruments that release high frequency and tones like flutes and violins. On the other hand, if you want to represent the majesty of God, you might play drums, bass and possibly low tones on a piano to release frequencies that represent the power and majesty of the King upon His throne. Having said this, within the scale of what is available to our senses through sound, I believe that it's possible to release a symphony of sound that represents and communicates the symphony of the very nature of God.

The Science of Worship

Ephesians 5:19: "*Speak to one another with psalms, hymns and spiritual songs. Sing and make music in your heart to the Lord.*"

In this Scripture, the phrase translated "*make music*" comes from the Greek word psallo. Psallo means to touch or strike the chord, to twang the strings of a musical instrument so they gently vibrate.[2] Our hearts have the ability to be "*played*" by both God and ourselves. We have already discussed the fact that God is light, that light and sound are of the same substance, and so therefore God is sound. I propose that God communicates revelation to us through sound, through vibrations. The amazing thing that I am trying to convey here is that God does not only generate and release vibration, HE LITERALLY IS THE VIBRATION. The human heart, the very center of physical and spiritual life, is both a tonal receiver and generator. For example, when God wants to release peace to us, God resonates the very part of Himself that is peace within our hearts. Our spirits receive this vibration and it eventually disperses throughout our mind, will, emotions and even our physical bodies. Ministry to others is essentially the transmission of what God is resonating within us to others. Most of the time, instead of using tones to communicate to others, we use music, words, movement and art.

But people are still able to literally pick up on others' tones. Have you ever used the phrase when describing someone, "*I really like that person's vibe.*" The word vibe is not just a catch phrase, but a literal scientific and spiritual truth.

You may have heard it said that music is the universal language. Music is the universal language because it is able to transcend the use of verbal language and invoke states of mind within those that come into resonance with the tones that are produced. Music is essentially able to create unity in the resonance of God as we translate the resonance in our hearts, from God, into the atmosphere through vibrations in the air that reach the ears that vibrate and send the signal to others. God can literally use a single musician to communicate His TONE to a group of others. God plays the heart of the musician who in turn plays the instrument as a translating device in order to communicate those vibrations to the hearts of men. We literally re-present the vibrations of God when we present music that originates from God.

Worship is our response to the revelation of God that we receive through His reverberations. Worship through song and movement is the physical declaration of the echoes of our heart released unto the Father. This is the worship the Father seeks, worship from our spirit, truthfully ours. You are releasing the melody of your heart back to the Lord as you worship through the vibration of your vocal chords and the movement of your body. You can re-create and translate the vibrations of your heart into forms of music, singing and movement in response to the Lord.

The Point of Transcendence

Have you ever been in the midst of worship and felt as if you had shifted into another realm? Sometimes it happens and you don't even realize it. Other times you can literally sense that you are moving from one realm to another. As triune beings, we are made up of body, soul and spirit. Although I can sense God both in body and soul, my desire is to ultimately connect with God in the spirit. If we are at all honest with ourselves, we must admit that we are limited in how much we can connect with God through our physical bodies and minds. There is a place God desires to take us that goes beyond our finite senses. I want to acknowledge that the word transcendence does have New Age connotations in our culture. That said, I choose to use the word transcendence to describe the transition from our carnal minds into our spirits and eventually into the mind of Christ.

I want to share a vision with you that the Lord showed me when I was ministering in Missouri. I was playing the piano and I could sense that the people in the room were not engaging into the presence of God because they were thinking too much. Many times we miss what is happening in the Spirit because we try to figure things out instead of trusting the Holy Spirit of the Lord. As I continued to play, the vision began to unfold and the first thing I saw was a hurdle, the kind of hurdle you would see at a track and field event. After the hurdle I saw a large brain. People were running and jumping over the hurdle and landing onto the large brain. What the Lord began to reveal to me through these visuals was that people needed to learn how to overcome the hurdle of their own minds in order to jump into the mind of Christ. The large brain that I saw represented the mind of Christ. Oftentimes we need to overcome our own limited minds in order to flow into the spirit and into the thoughts and insights of Jesus Christ.

Transcendence is the process in which humans move beyond the immediate time, place, and circumstances, and transport to places and concepts of meaning, enlightenment and inspiration.[3] David Aldridge states that, "*As a process, transcendence is seen as taking us beyond our small selves, out-*

side the everyday limitations of personality."[4] I believe that coming into the presence of the Lord is a matter of our choice to enter in to what God is continually presenting to us. This transcendence is not that God enters into our space but rather that we become aware that we are dwelling in His.

Jesus Valued the Alpha Wave Brain State

Saying that Jesus valued the *alpha wave brain state* is another way of saying that Jesus valued times of silence and solitude. I want to share two such instances as shown through His life in the book of Luke.

Luke 5:12-16 records the story of Jesus healing a man with leprosy. Although Jesus asked the man not to tell anyone of his healing, the news spread and the great crowds appeared. Yet, in the midst of all this, we find that Jesus often withdrew to places of silence and solitude. Jesus needed times of refreshing for the rejuvenation of His body, soul and spirit.

Luke 6:12-13 shares the account of Jesus choosing the original twelve apostles. Before doing so, Jesus spent the entire night in prayer upon a mountain. Jesus knew the value of silencing Himself to take council with the Father before making important decisions.

There are physical states of mind in which we receive revelation and creative thought more than other states. There are different levels of frequency that the brain emits that put us into different states of thought, states that we can purposefully choose. The first level of frequency I want to discuss is beta. Beta frequencies (above 12 Hertz) coincide with our most *"awake"* analytical thinking. For example, if you are solving a math problem, your brain is working at beta frequencies. I was astounded to discover that most of our waking hours as adults are spent in the beta state. This means that the average person, from the time they crawl out of bed until the time their head hits the pillow, spends all of that time in an analytical state of mind. The problem is that this *"beta state"* is often the place of analyzing, wondering, worrying and doubting.

The next lowest state of frequencies is called *alpha*. Alpha frequencies range from 8 to 12 Hertz and are commonly associated with relaxed, meditative states. I refer back to my point that Jesus valued this alpha wave state, and so I believe we should also. Listen; when I begin to play music during a meeting and people go from a place of hustle and bustle into a place of peace in five minutes, it's not just an accident. I'm representing the sounds of heaven so that people can come down from their beta states and into a lower, relaxed state in which they can begin to more effectively meditate upon the realities of the Word of God. By the way, meditation is not a *"new age"* word, it's an *"original age"* word found all over the Bible.

The fact is that we all need to purposefully make time to descend from our analytical states of mind into places of peace, discovery and insight. I believe that when Jesus went away into the places of solitude, He was keeping himself aligned with the Kingdom of God. He was getting away from the city and the bustle of the crowds to be rejuvenated in the presence of His Father.

The last state I want to discuss is the *theta state*. Frequencies below 8 Hertz are considered theta waves and are most associated with creative, insightful thought. There are plenty of people who want answers to life's question. We all need continual wisdom—directional wisdom—for our lives. Let me tell you that you most often will not find any of this in your analytical mind. For example, there are instances during our Rejuvenation Gatherings where people will get wisdom and insight on things that they have been trying to figure out for months or even years. This is just one instance that shows that there is great value in taking the time to silence ourselves in the presence of the Lord in order that we may hear what the Spirit of the Lord is saying.

Tuning Out the Noise — Tuning In to Specific Frequencies

What we call *clarity of sound* is simply the elimination of noise, which thereby allows us to resonate with the frequency of the Word of God. White noise is the fullness of the sound spectrum represented all at once just like white light is the fullness of the color spectrum presented in unison. When people come into a Rejuvenation Gathering, the goal is to eliminate unwanted noise in the lives of people so that they can focus in on the word God wants to specifically speak to them. There is a sound in the midst of the white noise that God wants us to focus in on. Just like you can take a prism and break white light into colors and segments, I believe that hearing the *"Still Small Voice"* is the act of focusing in on the one segment of sound that God is emphasizing. This thought gives new meaning to the phrase *"tuning in."*

In the following passage of Scripture, the prophet Elijah had an experience in which sound needed to be eliminated in order for him to hear the voice of the Lord.

I Kings 19:11-13: The Lord said, *"Go out and stand on the mountain in the presence of the Lord, for the Lord is about to pass by." Then a great and powerful wind tore the mountains apart and shattered the rocks before the Lord, but the Lord was not in the wind. After the wind there was an earthquake, but the Lord was not in the earthquake. After the earthquake came a fire, but the Lord was not in the fire. And after the fire came a gentle whisper. When Elijah heard it, he pulled his cloak over his face and went out and stood at the mouth of the cave. Then a voice said to him, "What are you doing here, Elijah?"*

The four universal elements are water, wind, fire and earth. All the frequencies of the sound spectrum can be heard in these elements.[5] Three of these elements are mentioned in this passage in I Kings. Elijah encounters the sounds of wind, earthquake and fire but was not able to find God within them. The spectrum of the frequency that was released was so vast that Elijah was unable to focus in on anything specific. It was only after these things subsided that he heard the gentle whisper of God.

I believe that hearing God sometimes has more to do with silencing noise than it does with actually listening for God. Focusing on something specific is easier to do when you can eliminate unwanted noise. White noise drowns out specific noise by matching the frequency of the specific and by adding multiple frequencies around it to cause the specific to become just one of many. Your word from God can become literally lost in a crowd of noises.

Tuning into God is not a one-time experience to be had but a continual experience to be maintained. We have the choice whether or not we will align ourselves with the sound of heaven. Whether negative thoughts enter your mind from people you are in relationship with, the media or the father of lies himself, they're all noise when compared to the speaking word of God. Kairos *"now words"* come to those that wait upon the Lord.[6] When you make time to hear His word, God will then tune you in to the frequency of His word and it will become part of you because you now live and move and have your being to the tune of His word. You will literally vibrate like God vibrates on that issue. God's resonating word within you literally will change the way you live your life and carry yourself. This is why the practicing of the Selah is so important. The Selah, which means to pause and think upon, allows for words to flow from knowledge in our minds into the vibrations of our hearts.[7]

Dismiss the Negative Sound

Matthew 9:23-26: *"When Jesus entered the ruler's house and saw the flute players and the noisy crowd, he said, 'Go away. The girl is not dead but asleep.' But they laughed at him. After the crowd had been put outside, he went in and took the girl by the hand, and the girl got up. News of this spread through all that region."*

I find it interesting that Jesus put this crowd out and then proceeded to do this miracle. The mention of flute players is significant in this passage because these musicians were there to actually increase grief through the playing of their music. They were most likely playing a dirge, which is a lament for the dead.

When Jesus addressed the crowd and the musicians he was essentially saying, *"Quit playing that song and get out of here, because that sound does not line up with the reality that this girl is ALIVE!"* Jesus dismissed this negative sound and then spoke KINGDOM REALITY in its place.

Oftentimes negative words and sounds linger around us to the point that they conceal actual reality. I believe Jesus dismissed the song of lament and the sound of the mocking crowd in order to change the negative atmosphere in that room into an atmosphere that lined up with the reality of the Kingdom of God. It's important to realize, especially as those who minister through sound/music, that people are continually under the influence of negative words and sounds throughout the course of their daily lives. I consider it a blessing and great opportunity to be able to create an atmosphere through music in which these negative sounds are silenced and dispersed in order that people may be ministered to by the presence of Christ and the reality of His Kingdom.

Not Quite Ready for the Throne Room

It has been a challenge at times to know how to best lead others into the Throne Room of God. In my early years of leading, I would often try to rush people right into *"the deep stuff."* I wondered why people were not just ready to jump into the Holy of Holies!

A study of sound has given me an answer. The truth is that we literally can get to the Throne Room quickly, the access is there. It just takes time to line ourselves up with the frequencies of higher revelation once we've been exposed to the grind of daily living. People often walk into church coming straight out of work, traffic and cars loaded with kids, not quite ready to just jump into the *"deep side of the pool."* In my youthful zeal, I did not understand this but I've learned over the years that a progression towards the depths of God is often necessary. Just because there is a progression does not necessarily mean it has to be drawn out. I have no problem entering His gates with thanksgiving and His courts with praise. It's just that I would personally like to spend more time in the throne room than in the courtyard.

I put this progression theory to the test at one of our ministry gatherings. The Lord led me to do this as an example of how we respond to music and frequency. On the color spectrum, the color red has a lower frequency than blue and violet. Thus, the relative tone of red would be of a lower frequency than the sound or tone of violet. When you study colors and their meanings as it pertains to the Word of God, red is representative of the blood of Jesus and access to God. It's by the blood of Jesus that we have an access point or entryway into the very throne room of Father God. When you study the color blue, it speaks of revelation and violet/purple speaks of royalty.

Think of the progressive color spectrum R.O.Y.G.B.I.V - Red, Orange, Yellow, Green, Blue, Indigo and Violet. Now visualize red as both a color, a low note and as the entryway into the progression to the throne room of God. Now, as you progress from left to right along this scale, you will progressively move closer towards purple, towards a higher frequency and towards revelation of royalty.

To demonstrate this in our experiment, I had my good friend Nic Billman play the piano on the upper octaves of the piano. I stopped him after about twenty seconds. I explained to the people that we would go back into playing these high notes again, then I asked that Jon, the bass player, hit the lowest C note that he could play. Andy, the drummer, then began to hit the bass drum and toms and Nic hit a C note on the low end of the keyboard. I then led the band into a higher level of dynamics, and I began to cry out for a breakthrough in the atmosphere. Though it was an example, the people could not help but sense a shift in that place. What was happening was that the low sound frequencies were helping the people break through into the awareness of the presence of the Lord. There are many times when I minister and don't sense that we as a group are entering into the potential of God's presence, so I begin to engage in what many describe as *"warfare music."* Warfare is a term that some circles of the church have given to intense, dynamic music. I think the warfare taking place has less to do with coming against evil spirits and has more to do with getting ourselves opened up to the Spirit of God. This is breakthrough music. This is low-frequency, entry–point, RED music. After doing this for about a minute I had everyone stop except Nic, who then began to play on the high end of the keyboard again. This time, people were amazed at the difference between this time Nic played on the high notes versus the last time. The people were better prepared and positioned for the high level of frequency the second time Nic played, and they were better able to enter into these higher realms. Some of the people actually laughed in amazement that what I had talked about was actually proven true by our "*experiment.*"

To sum this up, what happened was that the low-tone music created a breakthrough that got all of us started on a progression towards places of higher frequency and revelation. Once the people got engaged in that place of breaking through, they were then able to progress even further into higher levels of frequency and revelation. I have done what I just described hundreds of times without people knowing what I was doing. I just think it's powerful when people actually have an understanding of how this all works, because knowledge helps you to engage. Knowledge helps you understand that these things don't just happen by accident. One thing the Lord showed me while I was demonstrating this is that sometimes we need to progressively work up to new levels of frequency or revelation. If frequency is like a series of waves and each wave a level of revelation, you can't just jump into high levels of frequency right away because you probably are not ready for it.

It was through understanding all this that I really began to realize why people are not ready to jump into the throne room from the first note when I start ministering. There are times when I create atmospheres of breakthrough and I can tell that some people don't understand what I am doing. Some people in the room join in with the breakthrough and some people don't. Eventually everyone enjoys the result, and the people that did not engage in the breakthrough still get to enjoy the result of the peaceful sense of the presence of God.

We Exist Because of the Word God Is Speaking

Modern science now shows that geometric rhythms lie at the center of atomic structures. When Polish physicist Andrew Glazewski carried out research into atomic patterns, plants, crystals and harmonics in music, he concluded that atoms are harmonic resonators, proving that physical reality is actually governed by geometric arrays based on sound frequencies. In other words, the foundation of life is a sound! Scientists used to think that the smallest particles in the universe were atoms. Then they discovered electrons and protons. Next came quarks. Now scientists have discovered something they call strings. These look like tiny pieces of spaghetti, except millions of times smaller. They vibrate just like strings on a violin or guitar but at a fantastically high rate of frequency. If the scientists are correct, that means that one of the most fundamental particles in the universe is a vibrating string.[8] These strings vibrate in response to sounds that God released at the point of creation, sounds that continue to resonate even now, sounds that hold together the very fibers of your being.

Andrew Glazewski, who was also a Jesuit priest, spent almost half his life studying musical harmonics as well as infrasonic frequencies. *"Atoms are known to be harmonic oscillators,"* he wrote, *"the nuclei being the oscillators themselves, the electrons and their orbits being seen as the reverberations and echoes of the periodic harmonic motions of the nucleus."* In Glazewski's terms this is *"the music"* of the atomic scale. Glazewski further found that there is a sonic field that emanates from the human body and differs with each individual as radically as fingerprints. One could further state that all physical reality could quite accurately be thought of as music/sound that has taken on form. Our bodies, in this context, are constantly releasing vibrations and music as distinct and unique as anything in the universe, singing and pulsating to their own rhythm.[9]

God sustains life by the vibrations of His Word that He spoke. When God releases a word and a sound, this word continues to speak. This is why God is able to watch over His word. His words are never fleeting. Once He speaks it He can't take it back. It is released for all time. That is why God can't lie because His Word cannot be taken back. We have the potential to tune into His word, to align ourselves with what already exists because the vibrations of His Word continue to speak. His words are NOW, but we are not always *"walking in the Garden."* We are not always aligned with the vibration of His Word.

We need to learn how to resonate with God. The word resonate is derived from the word resound and means to sound again.[10] Staying in step with the Spirit of God is simply being an instrument that resonates or re-sounds the sounds, vibrations and frequencies of God's living Word. Matter is organized by waveforms and frequencies. If you were to take two violins that are tuned exactly the same and pluck a string on one of the violins, the plucked string will produce a field of sound energy that will trigger the other violin's matching string to begin to vibrate and produce the same sound. This is called *"resonance,"* and it happens naturally.

Resonance is a basic principle that affects everyone and everything, all the time. This same principle applies for a person in need of physical healing or emotional transformation. The correct frequency reminds the body's energy field of its original blueprint, and brings it into harmony. When we are in the presence of a person who is expressing joy, the energy field of their joy brings our own joy to the surface, so we resonate together. This is true of other manifestations of this principle, in both positive and negative ways.

When a minstrel plays his or her instrument and releases the frequencies of the Kingdom of God, people in that atmosphere have the opportunity to align themselves with the literal frequency of the Word of God. My goal during the Rejuvenation Gatherings that I host is that people will leave tuned in the areas of their lives that they were out of tune in when they walked into the meeting.

Sound Created and Maintains Creation

I remember the first time my wife showed me a video on the Internet that showed scientists placing sand upon metal plates and then vibrating the plates with the use of a tonal generator. These videos can be found all over the web, but I still marvel every time I watch one. When the sand sits on the metal plate before the tonal generator is turned on, it sits in a shapeless pile. Once the tonal generator turns on, the sand begins to take the shape of a geometric pattern. The amazing part begins when they start turning the tones up to higher levels of frequency. As the frequency goes to the next level, the sand actually moves into the form of a totally new geometric shape. This transition of shapes continues to occur as the tones are increased in frequency. It's interesting to note that the higher the tone gets, the more complex the geometric shape gets.

Genesis 1:2 says, *"The earth was without form and void..."* Then God spoke! Then God released a sound and creation took place. The sound that God released in Genesis is the very thing that not only created life but that also continues to sustain it. God spoke to dust and it resonated into the form of a man. God's sustaining word is the *"tonal generator"* that holds the very fiber of our being in place. Have you ever wondered how trillions of atoms all hold together and keep the shape and form of your body? It's the word/sound/vibration of God! Many of us are familiar with Acts 17:28 which says, *"For in Him we live and move and have our being."* The Bible in Basic English translation says, *"For in Him we have life and motion and existence."* Jesus said (in Matthew 4:4) that, *"man shall not live by bread alone, but by every word that proceedeth out of the mouth of God."* (KJV) The word proceedeth is not past tense, but present tense. Man lives and is sustained and held together by the word — by the sound that God is speaking NOW. I believe that if God ceased to speak, that the Universe would disintegrate! All that we know as creation is held together by the very word of God. God's word is the creator and maintainer of creation as we know it.

Dr. Hans Jenny is well regarded as the father of cymatics, which is the study of visible sound and vibration. He made use of crystal oscillators where one could change the frequency or amplitude of sounds, at will, and his invention of the tonoscope enabled human voice resonances to be made visible, without the intermediary of any electronic instruments. With his invention you could see the visible images of a song or a spoken vowel. Not only could you hear a melody, a letter, a vowel or word — you could see it! Now readers, I want you to read the following carefully because this is going to blow your minds! Many scholars concur that the Hebrew alphabet originated not from any man, but from God himself. Through Jenny's study of cymatics and the use of his invention, the tonoscope, he was able to prove this true.

When someone would correctly pronounce out loud, through Jenny's tonoscope, a Hebrew character, **it would take on the shape of the character**. Both Stan Tenen and Dr. Hans Jenny independently revealed this fact. Hans Jenny recorded the vocal expression of the letter on a plate of sand. The vibrations in the voice pronouncing the Hebrew letter caused the sand grains to take on the actual shape of the Hebrew character!

The Hebrew alphabet is a manual for creating matter; it is a sacred language that has been intentionally designed. The third book of the Kabbalah, the 'Sephir Yitzirah,' mentions the story of God taking letters from the alphabet to create the world. For centuries people ridiculed this idea and believed it to be a myth, but only now that we have reached scientific maturity can we marvel at these words, as indeed the Hebrew alphabet seems to be the blueprint of matter![11]

As we have already discussed, God's Word is not past tense but present. When I host Rejuvenation Gatherings and we create places for people to hear the word of the Lord, we are not just talking about hearing God say, "*I love you, man.*" The word from God I'm talking about is the Hebrew word *Dabar* which means to "*get behind and drive forward to completion.*"[12] In essence, the atmosphere created by the prophetic minstrel allows God's people to come into His presence to receive a guiding word that will drive them into the completion of their destiny in God.

God desires to transmit His re-sounding word constantly into His people. What is the re-sounding word? It's the word that sounds over and over and over again until it completes the purpose for which it was spoken. When I was called into the ministry of the minstrel, I received many words after my initial word. Some came to my spirit direct from the Lord and some came from others that spoke confirming words. God continued to resound His word in me in order to drive me forward into the completion of the word until it became a reality in and through my life.

The Power of Death and Life Is In the Tongue

The *Message* translation of Proverbs 18:21 reads: "*Words kill, words give life; they're either poison or fruit—you choose.*"

Many of us have heard of studies done by scientists regarding playing different forms of music to plants in order to monitor their growth in response to their exposure to the different genres of music. For the most part, plants exposed to classical music showed the most significant positive response to music. Oftentimes the plants exposed to classical music actually began to tilt towards the speakers from which the music was played.

I want to share a dream with you regarding this that I feel was from the Lord. I'm sure I dream more than I realize, but I rarely remember my dreams. When I do remember them, they are usually dreams that I know are from the Lord. This is one of those dreams. I remember walking into a room that contained a shelf holding several pots containing various types of flowers. As I approached the flowers to get a better look, I realized that all of them were beginning to wilt and wither. What I did next in the dream was I began to sing to the flowers. I began to sing notes and sounds; I did not sing specific words. As I began to sing, the flowers began to grow and bloom before my eyes. I literally sang the flowers back to life. Next I was in a large field approaching a stage. The stage was set up as if it were ready for a concert of some sort with microphones, speakers, etc. Hundreds of people were gathered in the field waiting for me to step onto the stage. Just before I began to sing on stage I awoke from the dream.

It was obvious what the Lord was speaking to me through this dream. There is an anointing with the minstrel through their voice and instrument to prophesy life directly into people. People will be literally restored back to fruition when the minstrel plays and sings over them.

Surroundings Affect the Nature and Expression of Your Being

In his book, *The Spell of the Sensuous*, ecologist and philosopher David Abram explores how those living in a sheerly oral culture, without written texts, became attuned to the *"voices"* of nature, so closely attuned that the very sounds of their own speech — its *"rhythms, tones, and inflections"* — reflected *"the contour and scale of the local landscape, the visual rhythms of the local topography."*[13]

My wife had the pleasure of being taught the Hula by one of our amazing Hawaiian friends, Kealoha. When you begin to understand what some of the movements of Hula mean, you realize that the movements of the dance pertain to the actual movements of that which they are describing. For example, the ocean waves are described in the dance with wave-like movements of the hands and arms. This is an example of how the very landscape that surrounded the native Hawaiian people influenced their communication through movement.

Our surroundings affect our movements and the very tones of our speech. Oh that we would remain in the realms of the Spirit of God and allow the atmosphere of His presence to affect our very expression through the course of our daily lives! The Word of God says that the name of Jesus is like a fragrant perfume poured out (Song of Solomon 1:3). When we linger in His presence, the fragrance of the name of Jesus gets on us and it has a positive effect upon others everywhere that we go.

Take Time to Listen for the Sound

In recent years I have really enjoyed studies regarding the relation that the science of sound has to the person and presence of God. It's inspired me to gaze further into the potential of His presence. It has motivated me to pursue things that I previously did not know were available. My hope is that you would stop and consider, the next time you hear music, that there may be something more to it than you once realized.

Strong emotional connection with music, and ultimately the presence of God, is not something that usually emerges when we just happen to be around some background music. The depth and authenticity of the feelings that music summons up are often related to the carefulness with which we listen.[14] People that go deep and wide in God don't get there by accident. They pursue God with passion, expectation and purpose. May we all pursue the person and presence of the Lord beyond what ears hear and what eyes see.

---

[1] Ray Hughes, *Sound of Heaven, Symphony of Earth* (Ray Hughes/Morningstar Publications, 2000), 11.

[2] Net Bible. Retrieved October 7, 2011 from http://classic.net.bible.org/strong.php?id=5567

[3] Lucanne Magill, *Music and Altered States* (Jessica Kingsley Publishers, 2006), 13-14.

[4] David Aldridge, *Spirituality, Healing and Medicine* (Jessica Kingsley Publishers, 2000), 38.

[5] Ray Hughes, op. cit., 27.

[6] Wikipedia. Kairos. Retrieved October 7, 2011 from http://en.wikipedia.org/wiki/Kairos

[7] Wikipedia. Selah. Retrieved October 7, 2011 from http://en.wikipedia.org/wiki/Selah

[8] Don Saliers, *A Song to Sing, A Life to Live* (Don Saliers and Emily Saliers/Jossey-Bass books, 2005), 30.

[9] The Power of Vibration. January 2006. Retrieved October 7, 2011 from http://www.learnmindpower.com/articles/power-vibration/printable/

[10] "Resonate." Oxford American Dictionary. 2nd ed. 2005.

[11] Science and the Scriptures. Retrieved October 7, 2011 from http://www.soulsofdistortion.nl/SODA_chapter11.html

[12] The Dabar of the Lord – The Kingdom Iconoclast. Retrieved October 7, 2011 from http://iconoclast.weebly.com/the-dabar-of-the-lord.html

[13] Don Saliers, op. cit., 56-57.

[14] Ibid., 71.

Chapter Six
Facilitating God's Presence

The Lord is stirring my heart about ways that the church might create corporate venues that are more purposefully made conducive to the spontaneous moving of both the Body of Christ and the Holy Spirit. I am in no way disrespecting the ways in which churches are currently formatting their gatherings. I am simply presenting some additional possibilities of how we might corporately seek and find the Lord.

As a minstrel, I have both acted as a facilitator of a meeting as well as a creator of musical atmosphere for other ministers to facilitate people to engage into the presence of the Lord. To have a team of leaders that are sensitive to the moving of the Lord is key to seeing that the entire crowd that is gathered enters into what the Lord desires to do in the moment. This requires a certain level of unity. I've always said that the best way for us, as the church, to be in unity is for each of us, as individuals, to be in unity with God first. When we are in unity with Christ, we will be in unity with each other. In the book of Acts, I believe one of the reasons that Jesus told the disciples to stay in Jerusalem and wait was so that they could slowly, but surely, get their own ideas out of their heads in order to receive what God had planned for them.

> Acts 1:6–8, *"So when they met together, they asked him, 'Lord, are you at this time going to restore the kingdom to Israel?' He said to them: 'It is not for you to know the times or dates the Father has set by his own authority. But you will receive power when the Holy Spirit comes on you; and you will be my witnesses in Jerusalem, and in all Judea and Samaria, and to the ends of the earth.'"*

In this passage, it is evident what was on the minds of the disciples. They were thinking about the restoration of the kingdom to Israel. Some of the disciples definitely had their own ideas about what Jesus should do and what should happen. Jesus goes on to tell them not to worry about that, but to wait for the empowerment of the Holy Spirit to be witnesses to the ends of the earth. At this moment, it is apparent that the disciples were not in tune with the plans that Jesus had for them and their future. This is one of the major reasons why I believe they were instructed to wait.

Waiting on the Lord is not only for the purpose of hearing His plans for us, it is also the time where the plans we have that are not His are laid down and submitted to Him. We oftentimes have to relinquish what we think before we can pick up and move with what God is saying. Unity happens in the midst of gathered Christians when we can all submit our own ideas to the Lord and wait upon Him for what He is speaking and instructing. Acts 2:1: *"When the Day of Pentecost was fully come, they were all with one accord in one place."* (KJV)

We need to look further into the meaning of *"being in one accord"* in order to understand the position we must take in order to more readily follow the leading of the Holy Spirit when we gather together.

The Greek word here for *"one accord"* is *homothumadon*, which is a compound of two words meaning to *"rush along"* and *"in unison."*[1] A unique Greek word, it is used 10 of its 12 New Testament occurrences in the Book of Acts and helps us understand the uniqueness of the Christian community. The image is like a musical metaphor: a number of notes are sounded which, while different, harmonize in pitch and tone.

This gives a different picture of unity than what most might be used to. We often think that unity means everyone is thinking and doing exactly the same thing. But as with the orchestral reference, although there may be different parts playing different things, there is a unison of many parts that occurs that brings a fullness of expression. This is the picture of the Body of Christ, a body of many parts, working in unison under one head, which is Christ.

Seeking — Discerning — Moving

Acts chapter 2 is one the most familiar passages of Scripture in the Word of God. This is the account of the original day of Pentecost. If you read the entire chapter with a focus on how the day unfolds, it is interesting to note the order in which things transpire. They started in the upper room seeking the Lord in prayer. They did not set up a series of meetings in order to preach the gospel; rather, they spent time together seeking the Lord. The Word goes on to tell us that they were filled with the Holy Spirit and they spoke in other tongues as the Spirit enabled them. This led to Peter preaching to the crowd, which ultimately brought three thousand into the Kingdom that day.

I reference this story as an example of how to facilitate the moving of the Spirit of the Lord. Peter was the facilitator in this instance. Peter was sensitive in discerning what was happening in the moment and he used his influence to steer the focus of the people towards the Lord. At first, people were laughing at those that had received the Holy Spirit, mocking them as if they were drunk. Peter's role, as a facilitator in this moment, was to draw the attention of man away from man and unto the Lord. Because of Peter's ability to facilitate the attention of others upon what the Lord was doing in the moment, I believe that the will of the Lord was accomplished on that day.

I sum up the day of Pentecost in this way: People sought God, God manifested, man discerned what God was doing and man facilitated the move of God. I believe that we can sometimes grow so familiar with this story of Pentecost that we forget the fact that those people in the upper room really had no specific idea of what was about to take place. None of them are recorded as specifically asking to speak in other tongues or seeking a sound like a mighty rushing wind. They simply waited on the Lord for what He wanted to do. God revealed Himself in the moment, the people discerned what the Lord was doing, and they then moved out upon that and facilitated the move of God and saw the will of the Lord accomplished upon that day and beyond.

Distractions from the Still Small Voice

I was recently doing a podcast interview with a great friend of mine, Pastor Josh Ellis. We were discussing the use of technology in church as a simple tool rather than that which draws people into a church. Josh brought up the story of when Elijah heard the *"still small voice"* of God.

Josh went on to say that none of the tools that we use in church are inherently wrong, but it is wrong when they become a distraction that keeps people from hearing the whispers of God. I totally agree with him. We can't allow things that are supposed to help aid us in experiencing God to end up distracting us from Him.

Some of you may be familiar with Pastor Mike Pilavachi and Soul Survivor Church in Watford, England. The worship leader at this church in the late 1990's was Matt Redman. During this era, God was really using various worship leaders in the UK to release worship songs in a fresh, new way. Despite England's overall contribution to the worship movement, Pilavachi's congregation was struggling to find meaning in its musical outpouring at the time.

Redman recalls, *"There was a dynamic missing, so the*

pastor did a pretty brave thing. He decided to get rid of the sound system and band for a season, and we gathered together with just our voices. His point was that we'd lost our way in worship, and the way to get back to the heart would be to strip everything away."

Reminding his church family to be producers in worship, not just consumers, the pastor, Mike Pilavachi, asked, *"When you come through the doors on a Sunday, what are you bringing as your offering to God?"*

Matt says the question initially led to some embarrassing silence, but eventually people broke into a cappella songs and heartfelt prayers, encountering God in a fresh way.

Before long, the church reintroduced the musicians and sound system. The people had gained a new perspective that worship is all about Jesus, and that He commands a response in the depths of our souls no matter what the circumstance and setting.[2]

I love that this pastor took the initiative to do what he did. He facilitated what God was asking him to do in that place and time. Here we see the importance of discerning and moving with that which God is revealing to us. The result was a congregation of people that grew in their understanding of what true worship is. People began to discover and release their responses of praise to God from the depths of themselves. This is what God desires to hear. In this instance, God was telling them to lay down the tools of a sound system and instruments for a season of time. It's amazing how even musical instruments can distract us from the Lord, but it can and does happen.

Tools and technology are great, but we must continue to live a life of worship when these things are not available. If our worship life does not exist outside the context of the tools and tech, we need to really ask ourselves if we are leaning too heavily on other things as they relate to our relationship with God.

Creators, Facilitators and Responders

As one who is used in the prophetic, I would often see things in the spirit during my time of preparation for a meeting. The Lord would begin to reveal to me things He wanted to do during the worship time. Often this would influence even the songs that I would choose for the time of worship. I would choose songs that fit the theme of what God was revealing to my heart. There were times when I was told that I *"preached too much"* during worship and that I should just sing the songs. I was struggling with trying to hold back the prophetic minstrel's function. Of course, I feel it is important to serve the vision of the pastor, and that is what I did. My frustration lay in the fact that I could never flow in what I did when I traveled while at my home church. I wanted to see my home church experience the things that we would see happen to those we ministered to on the road.

A minstrel creates atmospheres in which the moving of the prophetic takes place. So what do I mean by a *Facilitator*. Facilitators are very important in that they actually recognize what is happening in the spirit and encourage others to enter in. To define it, a facilitator is someone who helps a group of people understand their common objectives and assists them to achieve them. When you have an atmosphere creator and facilitator working together in unity, it is amazing what can take place in the presence of God.

The word minstrel comes from the word minister and can literally be translated *"little servant."*[3] The essence of the function of the minstrel is to serve others in order that they may encounter the power and presence of God. That is what motivates me to minister in this way. I find a sense of joy and satisfaction when I see others draw nearer to God as a result of the Lord using me to create an atmosphere for them to do so.

When I begin to sense the Lord wants to bring peace to His people during a gathering, I begin to translate that into the form of a song that resonates with a feeling of peace. I can actually create an atmosphere where people tune into the peace of the Lord that passes understanding. During this time I am acting as a creator. I am creating an atmosphere. When the atmosphere is apparent in the gathering, either I or someone else sensitive to the moving of the Spirit of God will begin to guide those gathered toward that objective God is bringing forth. Communication between creators and facilitators is very important.

There are different scenarios in which a minstrel ministers. One is that the minstrel creates an atmosphere and then another person, a facilitator, will convey this to the people. Another scenario is when the minstrel creates an atmosphere and then also acts as a facilitator to bring forth the word of the Lord. In essence I can both create an atmosphere for the prophetic and then also deliver the prophetic word though the song or spoken word. A third scenario involves the creation of a prophetic environment in which the church begins to facilitate what they are hearing over their own lives and towards one another.

I desire to facilitate gatherings in which the congregation understands, as individuals, how to position themselves to both hear the Lord for themselves and for others. As the minstrel creates an atmosphere, it allows people to be influenced solely by God and what His still small voice is speaking to them. I have run in to so many people that simply feel like they can't hear from God. This is simply a lie. Under the new covenant, we are all capable of hearing the Lord for our own lives as well as for others to bring encouragement, comfort and exhortation to them. I just want to be the minstrel that helps others to get away from the noise of life and into an atmosphere where they can be at peace and hear from the living God.

This is where the *Responders* come in. The responders are the church, the Body of Christ. Whether it is a word from one who is acting as a facilitator, or a direct word from the Lord, we need to begin to act upon what we hear. I remember once, during my Bible College days, one of the guest speakers was helping us to move out in releasing the prophetic. During the meeting, I looked way over on the other side of the room and saw a young guy, another student, attending the meeting. I felt the Lord impress on my heart that He was healing the young man of asthma right then and there and that I was to go and speak that healing over his body. Being somewhat new to this, I did what many people would do: I lifted my hand toward him from way across the room and prayed for him from there. It was amazing what the Lord did to prove to me that I was hearing His voice. Minutes later, the young man got up on the stage and gave his testimony that he no longer felt the symptoms of his asthma and that he had been healed during the meeting. The first thing I thought was, "AW MAN! *I missed my chance.*" But the Lord spoke to me gently that He wanted to show me that I really could hear His voice. Even though I did not fully obey the Lord that time, it encouraged me on my prophetic journey to step out more on the impressions the Lord placed in my spirit.

That guest speaker created an atmosphere for us that day. He told us that we could hear from the Lord if we would just position ourselves to hear from Him and to move upon what we heard. The minstrel does the same. The minstrel creates atmospheres in which people can encounter the presence, power and voice of the living God, Jesus Christ.

The Creation of Neutral Atmospheres

My desire is to continually learn how to encounter God in deeper and broader ways. In order to do this I have found that it often requires that I venture off of the written page and color outside of the lines. Please understand that I am not trying to throw prewritten songs out of our worship services. I write songs and I lead others in singing those songs. But these songs are really just what I call *"launching pads"* into the Spirit. Many of the songs I write are written for the purpose of taking people into a place beyond the lyrics that I am writing. In fact, the challenge of song writing is being able to whittle down what we, as artists, perceive in the moment of our inspiration to condense it into a few verses and a chorus.

The truth is, I have never really felt that any song that I've written did my original revelation justice. As an artist, I write songs about the Lord in order to attempt to capture the experience that led me to write the song in the first place. When I encounter the presence of the Lord in my own time with Him, I am presented with a facet of His nature that overwhelms me in that place. When I minister in music, the goal is to re-present to others what was originally presented to me. If I thought that reciting the simple lyrics of my song was enough to do that, I would stop there. But I know that it is not enough. The reciting of the lyrics is only part of the process of re-presenting what was originally presented to me by the Lord. The word represent literally means to *"present once again."* As a re-presenter of the living God, my desire is to try to help others come into the fullness of what was first presented to me. When I do this, I don't want to just stop with the reciting of lyrics, because I know that there is so much more to the picture. How do I know? BECAUSE I WAS THERE! I literally want to try to re-create the environment that I was in when I had my original revelation. I want to set a mood and create an atmosphere where others can have a deep measure of the encounter that I originally had. I am taking people to places in God that I have already been. When I encourage others to go beyond the lyrics, I am encouraging them to pursue more in God than the lyrical interpretation of my experience. I am helping others to have their own experience.

Again, I don't want those reading to get the impression that I am against using prewritten songs in worship gatherings. I am not against singing these songs, using PowerPoint and all the rest. I just believe that singing prewritten songs is only one way of experiencing God. When we make just singing these songs the focus of our worship gatherings, we often miss out on the full transaction of what real, relational encounters with our Lord can be. When I lead others in worship, I don't want the ultimate goal to be the recitation of my lyrical interpretation of what God presented to me. The ultimate goal of worship should be to create atmospheres that help others eventually have their own, personal encounters.

I personally believe that there has never been a song or song list created that touched the hearts and met the needs of every person that showed up at any particular worship gathering. That is why I believe we need to implement what I call "*Neutral Atmospheres*" into our services and meetings. These neutral atmospheres can be implemented for the entire worship time or for just a portion of it. As I define it, a neutral atmosphere in worship is created when minstrels create instrumental atmospheres that allow people to engage in the presence of the Lord without any external influences.

Neutral atmosphere allows people to engage in God's presence, receive direct inspiration and release spontaneous praise. I never want to become so dependent upon the external inspirations of song lyrics and motivational leaders that I don't know how to spontaneously praise or seek God anymore. The absence of spontaneous praise is a result of the absence of direct inspiration. If people are no longer directly inspired by the living God in churches to the point that they cannot sing a new song unto the Lord for thirty seconds, an adjustment needs to be made so that people can develop and grow in their first-hand inspiration and discovery of God.

Recently my wife and I, along with baby Zoey, were participating in a live, web-stream church service. We were enjoying the worship portion of the service. I was lying on my living room floor and Ann-Marie was dancing before the Lord with Zoey in her arms. I was really engaged in God's presence when suddenly they stopped the worship song and, before you could blink, the associate pastor was on the screen about to give announcements. Immediately I said out loud, *"I'm not finished and neither is God!"* and I pressed the pause button on the computer screen. I then continued to lead my family in a time of spontaneous worship! By pressing the pause button I created my own neutral atmosphere. I launched off of the worship songs that the church had been singing into a time of personal expression to the Lord.

I believe that one of the simplest forms of worship is a spontaneous response to a direct revelation. What worship has been often limited to is the repetition of second-hand revelation instead of the declaration of first-hand discovery. Of course, we are supposed to share our revelations with each other and encourage one another. But I don't want to live my life satisfied only with the revelations of others. I want to discover the depths of His presence first-hand, and so should you.

The Re-Presenters

The minstrel is anointed to re-present the songs and sounds of God. You can only re-present something that was first presented to you. Oftentimes a representation is also a translation of one's thoughts or words through an interpreter. I believe that all of us are, in some form or another, called to be representations of Christ. As a musician, I am called to represent the songs and sounds that the Lord puts in me.

When one prepares a sermon for a Sunday morning message, he/she will often study throughout the course of the week in order to prepare notes from which they will share. That is one way to prepare, but the preparation of the minstrel is different in that their time spent in the presence of the Lord is their preparation. It's a preparation of the spirit. It's not a time to figure out what you will say as much as it is a time to tune in to the One who will speak, Jesus Christ.

At a church I ministered at recently, the pastor asked me what was on my heart before the meeting started. I told him, *"I'm not sure yet."* I often don't know what is going to happen until I begin to create the atmosphere. Then I begin to hear and release in the moment. Don't get me wrong, there will be times that God speaks to me ahead of time, but it is never the fullness of what eventually comes out in the meeting. In reality, when I create an atmosphere, I am only doing what I am trying to encourage everyone else to do, and that is to sit before God, hear His voice and act upon that through the prophetic. Sometimes preparation means taking notes and filling ourselves with the Word of God. Sometimes it means emptying ourselves of everything so that we can be empty of our own initiatives in order that the Lord might flow in the way that He desires in the moment.

Musical Imagery, Imagination and Memory

I want to share some things from Carl Seashore and his book, *Psychology of Music*. The quotes I will share have such practical application to them for the minstrel.

The musician lives in a world of images, realistic sometimes even to the point of a normal illusion. He creates music by "hearing it out," not by picking it out on the piano or by mere seeing of the score or by abstract theories, but by hearing it out in his creative imagination through his "mind's ear." [4]

After musicians become truly familiar with their instrument, they can actually begin to move into a realm in which they hear what notes are coming next. I am not talking about practicing note for note and remembering which note comes next. I am talking about when you literally know what is coming next even though you have never played what you are playing in your life. It's an ability to play what you are playing yet in your *"mind's ear"* hear into the very future of the song and then play that which you have already heard in your mind when the time comes. As a prophetic minstrel, I believe that the Holy Spirit actually is resonating within me the notes and frequencies that He wants released, and then I release them through the instrument of my piano, voice or whatever else I may be playing.

The most amazing part about it all is that the world of images that I am tapping into is just as real as the one I am in. The realms of the Kingdom of God are available to my spirit so I can tap into them, receive them in that place and then translate them back to others through my instruments. This activity is in essence the summary of what I believe a true prophetic musical messenger is. We enter heavenly realms, remember it and then re-present it in the natural realm for others to enter in and join us in the spirit. Through my experience with both music and the presence of God, I am now at the place in my walk with God where I can move into these realms any time and any place. I have spent enough time going to these places in the presence of God to where I can both revisit places I have been as well as delve into new places in the Spirit of God.

Many of you have heard this quote before; *"You can't lead someone to a place that you've never been."* It is so true, and I believe this holds true for musicians that desire to lead others into the presence of God. There is a big difference between leading some songs versus attempting to re-create places in the spirit that they have previously been. Unfortunately I believe that there are worship leaders today that view their jobs as simply leading others in lyrical recitals, and it's really supposed to be much more than that. Here's another quote by Professor Seashore:

Without the warmth of the musician's experience, music would lose its esthetic nature. It's a well-known fact that many persons who ply the art of the business of music report having no developed imaginal life or concrete imagination. And it has been very interesting to observe in many such cases that, although they are engaged in the practice of music, their musical life is quite devoid of the genuine musical experience. They are often more pedagogues or musical managers.[5]

As musicians set apart to serve the Body of Christ and lead them into the presence of the Lord, we have a responsibility that is much greater than being *"musical managers."* There is more to it than getting together a list of songs. Many people in the music business view it as simply that, a business. They take their skills and abilities to play and use them to make a living but, when it comes to the church, there needs to be more to it than that.

The preparation of the musician in the church has a lot more to do with just getting the song list together. It is about spending time developing the imaginal life in the Spirit of God. It is about getting alone with the Lord and going to the place in the spirit that He wants to take you. It's only after that when we will be able to take others into those atmospheres. When people comment on how much they enjoy my ministry, they have no idea that it was rooted in years of solitude with the Lord. I only took them where I had been, and sometimes we go to new places together and I love when that happens!

One reason why I don't think some worship leaders in churches spend time in these places in the spirit is because leadership unfortunately does not require it nor do they make room for the release of it in a congregational setting. If it's not going to be released, then why should worship leaders spend time during the week preparing for what can't happen in the context of Sunday's liturgy? I totally understand this point.

It's true that you need three things in order to move with the Spirit of God in this spontaneous way during a congregational meeting. First, you need a willing leadership that will support the musicians in their efforts to follow the leading of the Holy Spirit. Second, you need musicians that have already been in the presence of the Lord, those that have experience seeking and finding God. Third, you need a people who understand how to seek and find God in these provided atmospheres. If any one of these three is missing in the context of a neutral atmosphere, the potential that is available will not fully be met.

I have been in meetings where I was willing and the people were willing but the leadership was not. I have been in meetings where the leadership and I were willing, but the people did not quite understand how to follow. But there are those times in which all three line up and we go into amazing places in God. I truly believe this is possible at all times due to the fact that God is ready for us. The big question is, *"Are we all unified in our readiness for him?"*

Has the Church Lost Their Spontaneity?

The Word of God clearly tells us to gather as believers in Hebrews 10:24–25: *"And let us consider how we may spur one another on toward love and good deeds. Let us not give up meeting together, as some are in the habit of doing, but let us encourage one another—and all the more as you see the Day approaching."*

There are so many ways that we can *"do"* church, as some say. I can't make a statement as to which way I think is the best way to do church because I personally believe that there shouldn't be one solitary way that we meet every time we gather. Once a group of believers are gathered, there are many ways in which they can conduct their time together. I am of the opinion that it would be beneficial to implement portions of time given to the spontaneous leading of the Holy Spirit during corporate church gatherings.

Some would argue that the emerging generation's desire for *"freedom"* is due to the reasoning that we are now living in a post-modern church era in which a young culture simply desires different practices than the generations before them. I would say this is probably partially true, but I also think that this generation desires to tap into something that the first centuries of the church had, and that is a spiritual spontaneity that seems to be lacking in many gatherings of the church. It's more than just a desire to do things differently for the sake of being different.

I want to share a quote from the book, Music and Altered States. Dr. David Aldridge shares:

Spiritual traditions, when made manifest in religious forms located in their varying localized cultural contexts, are simply ways for us to understand the purpose of our lives. These forms need to constantly be revised in performance and informed through intuition if they are to maintain any present-day reality. That is why many religious forms feel redundant and restrictive because they have achieved a verbal dogma that fails to encourage the intuitive wisdom of current performances. Once religions, or sciences, begin to say that this is the only way of gathering knowledge, then the way to personal experiential knowledge in obstructed.[6]

As I've studied church history, many of the sects that branched off from the institutional church did not do so necessarily because of rebellion, but because they had personally experienced more in the presence of God than was available to them in the presentation of the Institution. They branched off and met together because of their desire to come together and release their personal expression unto the Lord. They also sensed a presence of the Lord in their gatherings that they were unable to enter into within the Institution.

Please realize here that I am not anti-institution. I believe that it has and will continue to have a place in our culture for years to come. I just believe that we will meet a great need and fulfill a great desire in people by taking more time for the creation of atmosphere that will release the spontaneity of the people of God.

Let me say it another way, when I go to church I don't always want to know what is going to happen! There lies an excitement and anticipation in the unknown. There is still a lot about the person of Jesus Christ that I have yet to discover, and I want to continue to have opportunities to know Him more, both personally AND corporately.

Spirituality Versus Religion

I believe that there is a difference between spirituality and religion. I define religion as an act of formulating the forms or containers for spirituality as well as the means by which spirituality is attained. In other words, religion is man telling man what to believe about God and how to attain access to God. Religion tells you which spiritual practices are acceptable and which ones are not.

Traditionally, religions have regarded spirituality as an integral aspect of religious experience and have long claimed that secular (non-religious) people cannot experience *"true"* spirituality. Many do still equate spirituality with religion, but declining membership of organized religions and the growth of secularism in the western world has given rise to a broader view of spirituality. Secular spirituality carries connotations of an individual having a spiritual outlook, which is more personalized, less structured, more open to new ideas/influences and more pluralistic than that of the doctrinal faiths of organized religions.

At one end of the spectrum, even some atheists are spiritual. While atheism tends to lean towards skepticism regarding supernatural claims and the existence of an actual *"spirit"*, some atheists define *"spiritual"* as nurturing thoughts, emotions, words and actions that are in harmony with a belief that the entire universe is, in some way, connected; even if only by the mysterious flow of cause and effect at every scale.

In contrast, those of a more 'New-Age' disposition see spirituality as the active connection to some force/power/energy/spirit facilitating some sense of a deep self. For a Christian, to refer to him or herself as *"more spiritual than religious"* may (but not always) imply the relative deprecation of rules, rituals, and tradition while preferring an intimate relationship with God. Basis for this belief is that Jesus Christ came to free humankind from those rules, rituals, and traditions, giving humankind the ability to *"walk in the Spirit"* thus maintaining a *"Christian"* lifestyle through that one-to-one relationship with God.

In the midst of all this, I want to really encourage us all to realize that what sets us, as Christians, apart from the New Age movement and other religions is that, through our spirituality, we are relating to the person and character of Jesus Christ.

There are many spiritual practices that the Christian Church does not condone due to the fact that some of these practices are encouraged and taught by other religions. We need to be careful that we don't throw out neutral spiritual practices that can take us deeper in our walk with Christ simply because of their relation to other religions. To receive what I am saying, you must share my belief that practices like meditation are not inherently evil, but able to be used as spiritual tools to access either negative or positive. An example is that I can play a drum and tune into the presence of the Holy Spirit. A Shaman can use the same drum yet access a quite opposite spirit. Shamans view the sound of the drum as their horse on which they ride into the spirit world. I personally love this viewpoint. When you break it down, it's really not about the tool or instrument here. What matters is the spirit you are pursuing.

One thing that early missionaries failed at was their practice of removing a culture's spiritual practices as they simultaneously taught them who the real *"Spirit"* was. God created these cultures; in fact the cultures of the earth represent God himself. How dare we invade a culture and tell them that their cultural practices are an invalid way by which to worship the living God, Jesus Christ. When we do this, we are robbing God of that piece of His reflected nature that shines forth from that culture's worship. Sometimes I think that Western Missionaries forgot that the Bible says that God desires the worship of every nation, tribe, culture and tongue, not just theirs!

In his book, One Church Many Tribes, Richard Twiss states: *"Because we are all so prone to be culturally egocentric, the temptation is to consider our worldview the biblical and correct one, shunning all others as unbiblical and wrong. Worse yet is our habit of judging cultural ways—songs, dances, rituals, etc.— to be sinful when there is no clear violation of Scripture."* ⁷

Religion has more to do with a culture, whereas spirituality is more about the individual experience. William Irwin Thompson shares that, *"Religion is not identical with spirituality; rather religion is the form spirituality takes in civilization."* ⁸ I am not saying that religion is necessarily a negative thing, but it can become negative when the people involved are discouraged from pursuing God outside of the spirituality forms of specific religious cultures.

The Earth's Cultures Reveal the Nature of God

My wife and I have developed a love for many cultures, particularly Native American and Polynesian cultures. We have both ministered to and been ministered to by the amazing people of these cultures that are very different from what we were particularly raised in. As it pertains to worship, we found ourselves sometimes preferring the way that these cultures gathered together and related to one another. Now, through my recent studies, I have begun to understand why we were attracted to these cultures and their styles of worship even more than our own. The Polynesians, for example, have a much more laid-back approach to life in general. I am personally drawn to these people because I am a laid-back person myself. When I lived on the east coast for a few years, I was often told I was *"too laid back."* Of course, I thought all of those people were too uptight. As it pertains to worship and gathering as the church, I also prefer the laid-back style of the Polynesians' liturgy, if you can even call it that. It is so open and laid back that someone that is used to more structure in church would call this unorganized. I call it GREAT!

Don't get me wrong, there is a structure in these cultures as well, but I would describe their structure as more loose and open to spontaneity. I want to stress that what I am about to say is just my own opinion, but I believe that this open style of worship is closer to what God intends than the tight structure of many Western churches. All cultures, not just Western, tend to sometimes view their way of doing things as *"The Way."* Often this viewpoint is based in either pride or ignorance. I believe that all of us need to look into many cultures in order to perceive the bigger picture of The King and His Kingdom. Could it be that the Polynesian culture has a piece of the Kingdom culture that we as Westerners should pay attention to? Could it be that God is a little more open to spontaneity than we realize and that He is revealing that part of His nature through some of these other cultures?

I know quite a few of my Gentile brothers and sisters that have adopted the practice of the Friday evening Shabbat meal in their homes. I have attended several of these Shabbats in different homes with different families. Some of them simply gather together for a meal, and some of them light the candles and sing the traditional songs. None of these families are trying to be Jewish, but they have recognized and adopted a beneficial practice of another culture that is missing in their own. In the American culture where families are increasingly no longer connecting at the family dinner table, these families have instituted a weekly family gathering drawn from another culture.

I believe that in the arena of the practices of worship, it is beneficial to also look into the lives and practices of other cultures in order gain perspective into Kingdom Culture. Have you ever really stopped to think about what the music in heaven will be like? Do you seriously think that it's only going to sound like what's played on the local contemporary Christian radio station? It will be more diverse that what you can even imagine! I personally don't want to wait until heaven until I can tap into the diversity of the sounds of the Kingdom of God, and I don't have to.

One of my favorite times of worship took place in the nation of Wales. I was honored to lead a team of musicians at an event called *Celebration for the Nations*. We led worship under a large tent located on the *Llanelli Festival Fields*. I believe that there were over 40 nations represented, including a large number of South Koreans. I loved this experience because I was able to enjoy hearing and joining in with the worship of so many different types of music and styles in worship. One of my favorites was when the men's Welsh choir took the stage. They had to sing three encores because the Koreans kept giving them standing ovations. There were many times when the Koreans would lead in their own language and I could not understand the lyrics. I did not check out during their worship in the least because I understand that worship is more than the recitation of lyrics. I worshipped in the spirit and was able to experience God in amazing ways without having a clue as to the words they were singing.

The most memorable time of worship that my team and I led occurred during one of the afternoon sessions. As we were leading, all of the electricity to the tent suddenly went down. What's hilarious is that this is not the first time that this had happened to me while leading worship. Instead of stopping and calling it an attack of the devil, Andy continued to play on the drums. I ran off the stage and grabbed some bongo drums and we went off on a twenty-minute spontaneous drum-and-dance circle. In my memory, this was the most intense, joyous and radical time of worship during the entire week. All of these different people from different nations were moving and dancing and singing in their own way before the Lord. I can't even really describe to you what it was like except to say that I felt as if I was given a little glimpse into heaven that day. I am so glad the power went out!

Broaden the Structure to Broaden Expression

"Spiritual practices that people engage in often take place in groups that are guided by culture. As a cultural system, religion is a meaning-seeking activity that offers the individual and others both purpose and an ability to perceive meaning. We have not only a set of offered meanings, but also the resources and practices by which meanings can be realized." [9]

Culture is the practice of customs and traditions. Culture begins to vary when groups break off from others in order to increase or diminish certain practices and beliefs. We can study people and break them into cultures and subcultures, but each person that God has created has their own unique identity and potential for expression that nobody else has or ever will have. People are often stifled in personal expression because they will probably never be able to find an organization or culture that has created a structure that enables them to freely express the fullness of who they are. This oftentimes results in an individual's judgment of the organization and the organization's judgment of the individual.

Church splits throughout history have occurred because some group of people grew tired of the others group's expression of freedom or a lack of it. In order to create an environment for expanded expression of the people of the Kingdom of God, we are going to have to be open to creating more neutrality and thus experience more UNIVERSITY. Many of us are familiar with the term University as it pertains to schools of higher education. The word *University* literally is rooted in the joining of the two words *unity* and *diversity*.[10] Many think of unity as everyone doing the same thing at the same time. I believe the unity that God desires, the unity that those in the upper room had at Pentecost, is one by which all unique expressions are being released and unified as one harmonious response to the Lord.

Spirituality is going to be expressed through each individual in different ways. I believe this is what God intended in the first place. Organizations have created various forms of religion in which some people conform to the system while some *"rebel."* God intended us to meet together for the common good by which we all see in part and prophesy in part and walk in the ways in which God created us to express through our individual gifts with Jesus Christ as the Head of it all. I am not here to say that biblical structure, position and leadership are not in order. I believe in this, but I'm reminded of a quote from the movie Braveheart when William Wallace looked at the nobles and said, *"You think the people of this country exist to provide you with position. I think your position exists to provide those people with freedom. And I go to make sure that they have it."*[11]

We do not build churches so that people will attend to provide us with a position. We have been called to these positions by the Lord in order that we may serve the people by facilitating atmospheres and settings in which people are free to express their spirituality to God, receive from the manifest presence of God enthroned in that place and minister prophetic encouragement to one another. We need to stop calling people rebellious and out of order because they want to release their God-given expressions of worship that don't line up with a particular set of cultural rules.

Give Me a Venue

We were all created to be different from each other, and God did it on purpose. If we, especially as facilitators, are concerned with God receiving the unique expressions of all of His children, then we will make efforts to create venues in which these possibilities exist. God is too big for any one organization/form/structure of worship to be able to outline what aspect of Him is most necessary to view or the specific manner by which we should engage with His presence and express our worship.

After having read most of this book by now, you may be surprised by the fact that I actually enjoy many of the traditions of denominational churches. For years I've been attending the Christmas Eve service at a Lutheran church that my wife's family used to attend. They pull out the fifty-member choir, the forty-piece orchestra and, of course, the massive pipe organ. It's hard to stay seated in your pew as this team of singers and musicians belt out the first chords of *"Joy to the World."* My point here is that doing this once a year is a joy, but to do it every week would become monotonous to me. God is a diverse Person releasing diverse revelation and desires diverse expression of praise from a diverse body that He created.

I was encouraged when recently I came across a Baptist Church that is hosting evenings of contemplative musical prayer! I was really excited to see this. I want to share something that they put on their web site that essentially expresses what I believe that the church should consider doing in a greater capacity.

We invite you to worship and prayer in the custom of Taizé and Iona. This service of Contemplative Musical Prayer is a contrast to the traditional Baptist worship style. While we enjoy already rich worship and prayer traditions on Sundays and Wednesdays, the intent is to continue to expand opportunities to approach God, to open our hearts to God and to demonstrate obedience to God.

This prayer service is not intended to be a complete worship experience. It is not a replacement for a traditional worship diet, but a supplement to it. It is intended to enhance understanding of the nature of God and thereby to enhance ability to worship God in spirit and in truth.[12]

I LOVE THIS! My favorite part is, *"the intent is to expand opportunities to approach God."* This meeting on Monday night is not a replacement for the liturgy on Sunday morning, but an opportunity to supplement and add to other experiences that are offered.

I've prayed and asked God to release venues in which people can come and enter neutral atmospheres in which they can encounter God in the midst of their current circumstance. These venues are not just places where people will sing songs, but places where they will hear the songs God is singing over them, the songs of His Kingdom. It's a place to discover aspects of God's nature that become answers to their momentary needs. It's a place to be tuned into the vibrations of the heart of God. It's a place to release their Tehillah homemade praises unto the Lord within a neutral musical atmosphere that gives them the opportunity to do so. It is a place of expanded opportunity to seek and find the Lord in ways that vary from those that the liturgy of the local church has offered them.

My prayer is that the church will become a place that expands its facilitation of the presence of God. I believe it will lead to an increase of broadened experiences of relationship between God and man.

[1] Net Bible. Retrieved October 7, 2011 from http://classic.net.bible.org/strong.php?id=3661

[2] David Schrader. Song Story: Matt Redman. Retrieved November 5, 2009 from http://www.crosswalk.com/1253122

[3] John Southworth, *The English Medieval Minstrel* (Woodbridge: Boydell and Brewer, 1989), 3.

[4] Carl E. Seashore, *Psychology of Music* (Dover Publishers Inc., 1967), 5.

[5] Ibid., 6.

[6] David Aldridge, *Music and Altered States* (Jessica Kingsley Publishers, 2006), 13-14.

[7] Richard Twiss, *One Church Many Tribes* (Richard Twiss/Regal Books, 2000), 113.

[8] Wikipedia. Spirituality. Retrieved October 7, 2011 from http://en.wikipedia.org/wiki/Spirituality

[9] David Aldridge, op. cit., 164.

[10] Rick Joyner. Unity and Diversity. Retrieved October 7, 2011 from http://www.elijahlist.com/words/display_word/4519

[11] Braveheart. Mel Gibson. Icon Productions, 1995. DVD.

[12] Contemplative Musical Prayer Service. Retrieved October 7, 2011 from http://www.gambrellstreet.org/gsbclive/index.php/ourministries/worship/contemplative-musical-prayer

Chapter Seven

My Journey as a Prophetic Minstrel

My journey as a prophetic minstrel began in a very sudden and abrupt way. It was the spring of 1998 at the end of my first semester at Christ For The Nations Institute in Dallas, TX. One of my teachers invited the class to attend a prophetic presbytery. Our school held these presbyteries at the end of each semester in order to speak encouraging words of insight and blessing to the students. I had never been to a corporate gathering like this before and when I walked in, I saw two men at the front of the room sitting in chairs. They asked us to make two lines, and the men began praying and speaking prophetic words over those in attendance. There were also those that stood next to the men who were prophesying that were using portable cassette tape recorders to record individuals' prophetic words. For those of you that don't know, cassette tapes are devices that were used in ancient times to record voices for playback on a later date. After the word was spoken, they would hand you the tape so you could review what was said.

Even now, whenever I listen to the recording of the word I received, I can still picture that aging man sitting in his chair as he gruffly spoke in King James style, "*You shall know the fortifications of Zion. I say unto thee, the Tabernacle of David shall be restored and the Glory of the Lord shall come forth. You will have a minstrel's anointing and you will set many free and the Glory of my name shall be upon thee. So set at my feet for you are released and I will thrust you out with great thrust. Thou shalt defeat the strategies of hell.*"

I had wondered about music only a few times in my twenty years, but up until this night, I had never felt a serious desire to sing or play an instrument.

This word became a catalyst in my life that would propel me into a whole new arena of life. It's because of the fact that a prophetic word was so instrumental in the directing of my life that I believe so strongly in the prophetic ministry that I now function in.

Some of you might have expected me to tell you that I started my musical journey at the age of three and that I grew up singing and playing music my entire life. The truth is that I was not really interested in music at all while growing up. Being raised in a small Northern Illinois town, I was more interested in sports and the great outdoors. As a child, my greatest attempt at singing was when my dad *"gently forced"* me and my sister to sing *"And the Gift Goes On"* at Christmas time in the small, country, Methodist church we attended at that time. *I did it for you, Dad!*

As a young teenager, I began to sense a call to ministry upon my life. I knew that the Lord had set me apart for something, though I was not sure exactly what it was. I can remember spending hours in prayer during my high school days. Since we lived out in the country, I would spend a lot of time walking with the Lord along the dusty gravel roads just talking with Him. Many times, when my friends would actually venture out to my house to visit, they would find me in my room reading my Bible, writing sermons. Who I would preach them to, I had no idea. All I knew is that I had a strong desire for the Lord and His Word.

I did not grow up in a community of Christians that consistently demonstrated and moved in the prophetic gifts. We went to church and sang songs and listened to sermons, but I can't remember anyone in my church ever laying hands on me and speaking destiny over my life. In fact, I had to leave my hometown to find out what the prophetic was. The funny thing was, I was already moving in the gifts of the Spirit as a teenager. I was flowing in the prophetic, word of knowledge and word of wisdom. I now know them as the *"Revelatory*

Gifts." At the time, I had no definition for what I was doing.

When I received my prophetic word about a minstrel's anointing, I certainly had no definition for what it was. The presbytery took place in what was the Christ for the Nations Chapel at the time, which was located on the first of two floors in the building. The second floor was where the school library was located. I can remember heading up to the library after I had received this word in order to look up what a minstrel was. After looking for a while, I found nothing related to either minstrel or a minstrel's anointing. The only reference point I had to go off of was what a friend of mine at school told me a few weeks before the presbytery. We were in his dorm room when we got into a short conversation about music and the prophetic and I recall him telling me that he felt I might be a minstrel. I laughed it off. I had no idea what he was talking about or where he got such an idea. He got the last laugh because he was actually standing there with the prophet when he spoke the word to me. I think I can even hear him laughing on the recording with the tone of, *"I TOLD YOU SO"* attached to it.

I had no idea that the word spoken over my life that evening was the beginning of an amazing journey into the discovery of the minstrel's calling and anointing upon my life.

Conditional Prophecy

I want to mention two types of prophecy as it relates to seeing the prophetic word of the Lord actually come to pass. The first is known as the sovereign prophetic word. When the Lord speaks a sovereign word, it is released with definite power behind it. It means that no matter what, this word will take place. When we stand upon the written, logos word of the Lord, we stand upon its definitiveness and sovereignty. We trust that His word is true and steadfast.

The other is the conditional prophetic word. This type of word requires our participation to come to pass. The word may not necessarily come to pass if those it was spoken to do not join faith and action with the word to carry it out. I remember one of my pastors saying that if there is a promise there is most often a premise associated with the promise. Many people do not see the manifestation of words that were spoken over them and they become discouraged, thinking that they heard the Lord wrong or that the one who spoke the word to them was incorrect. On the contrary, I believe that many words are not fulfilled because we do not do what is necessary to work in conjunction with the Lord to bring them to pass.

When Jesus taught us to pray (Matthew 6:10), He uttered the words, *"Your Kingdom come, Your will be done on earth as it is in heaven."* I believe that we are able to bring forth that which is in the heavenly realm into the natural, earthly realm. I received a word from heaven, but it would take action on my part to bring it from the form of a word into reality.

Have you ever heard those testimonies about people that supernaturally began to play instruments within moments? Typically these stories involve people that at one moment had no musical ability at all, and then all of a sudden sat down and began to play masterfully upon an instrument. I really can't tell you how true those stories are. There may be those out there that have had this actually occur in their lives, and to those I say, *"Good for you. Now, to the other 99% of us...."* I like these stories, but what I don't like is when people hear these stories and then wait around for what they hear in these stories to happen to them. I have even had people ask me to pray for them so that they would be able to play the piano like I do. I chuckle and tell them it does not work that way. I will pray for you to have the tenacity to do something, but you have the ultimate choice to make it happen. In fact, the book you are reading right now was once just a word from the Lord in my spirit. I also had it confirmed that I would write this book by a prophet in the autumn of 2007. But it took hours of study, research, typing, re-vamping and gallons of chai tea lattes, thank You, Lord, to get it done.

From Word to Reality

Habakkuk 2:2-3, *"Write down the revelation and make it plain on tablets so that a herald may run with it. For the revelation awaits an appointed time; it speaks of the end and will not prove false. Though it linger, wait for it; it will certainly come and will not delay."*

This scripture in Habakkuk is my favorite concerning transferring things from the supernatural, heavenly realm into the natural. I am a huge advocate of writing down your dreams, visions and goals. I had always heard that it was a good idea to do this, but this scripture revealed a new level of importance to me when it came to physically writing down vision from the Lord. I have been writing vision down from the Lord for years now, and I have been amazed to see the results. Whenever I have written down vision that was truly from the Lord, I have seen it eventually manifest in the natural realm. There is a power in writing the word down and I believe this is why: **When you write a word down from the Lord, that is the first time that the word is actually manifesting into a natural form.** You may think it is just simply ink on a page or text on a computer screen, but it is so much more. Writing is a form of bringing the things of Heaven into the Earth. It allows you to see your vision, rehearse it, speak it, hear it, believe it and eventually achieve it.

I started school at CFNI in the spring semester of 1998, so I had the summer to think about the word that I received just prior to returning home. I thought about the things the Lord had spoken, and wrote out some practical ways that I could begin to move towards fulfilling it. I want to interject here to say that I was not simply stepping into all of this because a man gave me one word. I was moving upon the unction that I had within my spirit from God. I knew that this word was from Him. I did not really stop to question why He would wait until I was twenty-two years old to reveal this to me. I just took it, wrote it and ran with it. Today I am glad that I did.

I started my second semester in the autumn of 1998 with a whole new lease on the calling upon my life. Two of the major things the Lord told me to start doing in order to develop the calling on my life were to begin piano lessons and to try out for a worship team as a vocalist. I made it on to a chapel team, so I was able to develop in the areas of singing and observing how ministry was done in the context of a team of musicians.

I also began weekly private piano lessons. This is where I really began to discover that I had some hidden talent in my life. If you have ever had the thought that you might be good at something if you tried it, please do yourself a favor and try that thing! That may be one of the ways God is trying to tell you something about whom He created you to be. For some reason, I chose the piano simply because I thought I might be good at it if I tried. At first, I could not even hold my right hand in the correct position to play a chord. But I continued to make each lesson on time and I practiced for hours in between each lesson as well. I want you to realize that I did not just start playing the piano amazingly within weeks of starting. Although I do believe that some have more of a natural ability than others to play instruments, I do not believe that anyone is exempt from devotion to the development of your art form, whatever it may be.

The First Time I Sensed the Minstrel's Anointing

I want to fast forward with you now to the end of my third semester at school. By this time I had been through two semesters of private piano lessons with hours of practice logged in between. At some point in my second semester of lessons, something just clicked in me where I started to learn how to rhythmically feel music and sing as I played. This was not something I could do right away. I could not even sing the song I played at my first semester recital.

My practice times were not really conventional. They became my devotions. I would spend hours in those little practice rooms in the music building playing before the Lord. I was becoming a psalmist in those times. My heart began to pant after the streams of living water in new and expanded ways. I eventually began to write my own songs as I learned more about the structure of music. There was one song in particular that I wrote in that second semester that I really felt like I wanted to play for my recital. In only the course of eight months, I had gone from knowing absolutely nothing about music to asking my teacher if I could play a song that I had written for my recital. I was the only one at the recital that played their own song that semester; some had been playing years longer than I had been. I point this out to show that it is not about how long you have been playing as much as it is about how much you have developed yourself in the time you have been playing. I had followed the premises to the word the Lord had given me, and I was about to taste the first fruits of it.

The recital had come, and it was my turn to play. I got up and played just like I played in my practice room before the Lord. One of the things the Lord told me was that I was called to minister to Him first and that, when I would minister as His vessel before men, I should not allow others to influence me to change whom I was before Him. I sang and played with passion in the fullness of the skill that I had at that time. I remember hearing people begin to tear up as they heard the words and felt the atmosphere change in that recital room. This is the first time I can remember really sensing the actual function of the minstrel's anointing on my life. It had only been a year after the original word had been spoken over me, and here I was actually flowing in it.

Waiting on the Word

Very rarely will someone begin to move into the fullness of the vision that is within them right away. From the night I played that first recital, it would be years before I began ministering publicly. I spent more time developing my relationship with the Lord in the context of music and songwriting. It goes without saying that if you are called to speak on behalf of the Lord; you first need to learn how to hear His voice.

It was nearly five years from the time I received the initial prophetic word until I began a consistent public music ministry. Since that time, I have learned many things along the way. As I began public ministry, I never lost sight of the importance of getting away into the secret place with the Lord. The anointing of the minstrel comes from times in the presence of the Lord dedicated to devotion and intercession.

During those developmental years, I never felt in a hurry to minister before others. I knew there would come an appointed time for that. I knew that I needed to wait on the word that the Lord had spoken. I trusted that He who began the work in me would be faithful to complete it.

Walking In the Word

After you receive a word from the Lord, and after waiting for what can be years of standing on that word in prayer, there will come a time for a breakthrough. There will come a time when what you've been believing for manifests itself on the earth. It is a time of excitement and joy. It is also, oftentimes, just another beginning. Since entering the public realm of music ministry, I have ministered through music in many ways. I have played for hours in various worship and intercessory ministries. I have led corporate worship gatherings for both my home church and while traveling throughout the United States in conferences and meetings. I have taken teams to the nations and done exactly what I saw in my spirit back in school when I told others that I would have a prophetic team of artists that would travel to the nations. At this time, with all of the ministry that I, my wife and those that joined us have done, I believe we are only standing on the precipice of what the Lord is going to do.

During the summer of 2007, my wife and I led a team of musicians on a month-long tour through The Czech Republic and the UK. During this excursion, I began to notice a trend consistently occurring through our ministry. We seemed to be carrying an anointing that would produce atmospheres of rejuvenation and refreshing for others wherever we would go. I recall one such time of ministry that took place in the home of our hosts in Prague. I felt led to get the band together and we had the entire ministry leadership team from Prague sit down on couches in the living room. We then began to just play and sing over them for over an hour. It was a refreshing time for the team from Prague, and I felt so honored to be able to minister to them in that way. One of the things I thought after this was, *"I wonder how often this team of leaders actually receives ministry like this."* I knew for a fact that it was not very often, if at all. I also began to feel, through that experience, that to minister in that way as musicians was something that needed to become increasingly prevalent in the entire Body of Christ, not just in our ministry.

During the summer of 2008, we again were out ministering, this time in Honolulu, HI. (No *"suffering for Jesus"* jokes, please.) Our team had been ministering at a mission located in the area of the city known as China Town. Over the course of that week, we had ministered to people who came in off the streets. It was a great time, and we really bonded with the team that actually ran the ministry. I was impressed by the Lord that our team needed to gather the team from the mission into the office there so that we could minister to them. This team from the mission was amazing. Many of them were formerly in similar situations to those that they ministered to. By the grace of God, they were now at a place in their lives where they could minister to others. Over the course of the week, we saw how they poured out their lives to serve these people. This team ministered there week after week, some for years, and I knew they needed a time of encouragement.

I asked the leader of the ministry if we could get everybody up to the office. When everybody was there, we began to play music and sing over them. The prophetic unction began to well up inside of me and in others on our team. We began to sing songs of encouragement over the workers. My wife began to dance around some of the women on the team and tears began to stream down their faces. We laid hands on the men and encouraged them as brothers in Christ. Many of the mission team had never experienced anything like this. Again, I felt honored to encourage such laborers in the Kingdom of God. To be honest, almost anyone can come in for a week and minister at a mission like we did. But these were the dedicated ones who poured years of their lives into the ministry. We were able to strengthen and encourage them in what they were doing for the Lord.

The foundation of the prophetic ministry is to comfort, encourage and exhort others in the word of the Lord. There are so many teams of people like the leadership team in Prague, or the mission team in Honolulu's China Town that need encouragement along the way. I began to realize that a major part of our minstrel's calling was to use our gifts to encourage and strengthen others in the presence and word of the Lord. I figured that if I could not stay in a geographical location to make a long-time impact, the next best thing would be to strengthen those that could and that were.

Second Corinthians 1:3–4 says, *"Praise be to the God and Father of our Lord Jesus Christ, the Father of compassion and the God of all comfort, who comforts us in all our troubles, so that we can comfort those in any trouble with the comfort we ourselves have received from God."* God had brought a team of prophetic minstrels into that mission to pass on the encouragement that God had placed in us to give. The cycle continued that next day when that team passed it on to those that came in for a meal. And we believe that the cycle will continue, as those men and women come from the streets of China Town to the place where they will be set free to minister to others in the way that they were ministered to.

It had been ten years since that spring night at Christ for the Nations when I first heard the calling to the minstrel's anointing. In those years, I had ministered through music in churches, conferences and as a part of missions teams all across the United States and through the nations of the earth. But it had only been in the last few summers of mission tours that I really felt like I was tapping into the true minstrel's calling and anointing. In that living room in Prague and that office in Honolulu's China Town, we were able to freely flow in that calling and anointing.

I believe that in order to see the minstrel's anointing flow, there are certain conditions that need to be in place. These conditions involve a venue for release, an informed and expectant people and an anointed minister or ministry team. When we ministered to the mission team in China Town, we had the venue of the mission office. We had a place set apart for us to be able to freely flow the way the Lord wanted to flow through us. We also had a group of people that understood how we were about to minister and had their expectations set to be ministered to in a prophetic way. We told them that we were going to play our instruments to create an atmosphere conducive to the moving of the prophetic. They sat in chairs, closed their eyes and prepared their hearts for what was coming. They received from the ministry because they expected to. And, obviously, we were the team ready to minister.

The Release of the Minstrel

I believe that we are about to see a great release of prophetic minstrels to the worldwide Body of Christ. They will be fresh from the throne room of the Lord with the words of God's Kingdom in their hearts and upon their lips.

My observance is that, for a large part, the reality of the ministry of the minstrel has faded from the church. I have rarely observed anyone who has functioned in the calling and anointing of a minstrel. I don't think that this has very much to do with the fact that minstrels are not out there, because they are. I believe it has more to do with the fact that there is rarely a venue created for them to release this form of ministry. At one point in my journey I came to the realization that I was being called to function in a ministry that very few people had ever recognized or heard of. It is difficult to try to minister in what God has called you to minister in when people don't necessarily know how to receive from what you're doing.

Allow me to honestly share with you that there were times when I struggled not to take this personally. There were times when I felt misunderstood by leaders in my life and by the Body of Christ. What I had to realize was that it was not that they did not necessarily understand me personally, but the fact that they did not understand or recognize the minstrel's calling and anointing. As far as from what I could tell, there existed no platform for the functioning of this anointing in the church. There were times when I would try to function in the minstrel's anointing during a Sunday morning service or during a session in a house of prayer. Most of the time, it did not go over well because the people in attendance did not fully understand what I was doing or how they could posture themselves to receive from the Lord under that type of ministry.

I had to come to a place where I was not writing this book from a basis of trying to be understood by others. I needed to come to a place where I would write this from a desire to help the church to identify and receive from an emerging generation of prophetic minstrels, of which I am just one.

I believe I am called to be an advocate for the ministry of the minstrel. I am helping to prepare a way for others that are called to minister in this way. I believe that musicians that are identifying with the very things that I have been sharing are reading this. I recently received a message in response to a teaching on the minstrel that I released on my blog, *The Prophetic Sound Man*. The message was from a man in his mid-fifties. He wrote to let me know how much the teaching that I shared had impacted him. He went on to describe how the blog post had brought him to tears. He told me about how he had received a calling to the ministry of the minstrel back in 1983. Now, years later, he wrote to tell me that he felt as if his gift and calling had been squandered due to the fact that he had never found a venue to release his gifting within the structure of the church. Let me tell you that this man's correspondence lit a fire under me to complete this book and to release this message. I want to encourage the prophetic minstrels that your time of release is coming and even now has come. I also pray that leaders in the church will consider the value of the ministry of the minstrel in order that they may release them within their churches to function in this ministry.

Implementing the ministry of the minstrel is just another way of formatting our time together when we meet as the Body of Christ. It's creating venues and giving specific periods of time for people to directly hear from the Lord in addition to hearing sermons and teachings. I believe that leadership in the church requires the dual responsibility of both hearing God for others as well as helping others directly hear God. I don't believe that the speaking of the prophetic word will cease, or that sermons will never again be preached. I just believe that we are also called to teach people how to hear directly from the Lord and to facilitate atmospheres for them to do so.

I believe that the release of the function of the ministry of the minstrel is coming to a venue near you! My prayer is that pastors and leaders would consider the value of this type of ministry within their churches and ministries. I'm praying for venues to be released, places where atmospheres are created so that people can get the downloads from the Lord that they need in the moment. I'm praying for musicians to be set free from performance and released as servants of God and man in order that they may become translators for the release of the Kingdom Word of the Lord.

So, this is where I now stand in this story of mine. I stand at the precipice of possibility. The Lord has called me to educate, function and reproduce. I feel called to teach on these issues related to the anointing, calling and function of the minstrel. God wants to prepare people to realize who the minstrels are and what they are called to do so that they can receive what God wants to release through them. I also desire to see musicians released into this calling and function so that they can themselves bring influence to their spheres of society and culture. The minstrels are being released and my prayer is that they will be recognized and received for the glory of the Kingdom of God.

Chapter Eight
The Minstrels - God's Atmosphere Creators

While it is true that anyone, at any time, can enter into the presence of God, I believe that God has released the ministry of the minstrel for the purpose of serving others that they may be able to enter into the presence of God in the musical atmosphere created by the minstrel. When was the last time you heard the word minstrel spoken in a church? In a church that I recently ministered at, I asked the people to raise their hands if they knew what a minstrel was. Not one person raised a hand in that place! Instances like this have given me the desire to define who and what the minstrel is so that the church may be better informed regarding how to recognize and receive what God wants to release through them.

There are three terms most often referred to that are used to define ministers related to singing and music: worship leader, psalmist and minstrel. There are obviously many similarities between these three, but my goal here is to define these terms individually in order to reveal some differences between them. This is important to distinguish so that people who receive ministry by ministers functioning in these different anointings know what to anticipate. I've witnessed times when people have missed what the Lord was trying to accomplish through the minstrel because they were in a different mode of expectation. For example, when the minstrel is ministering, it is not a time to try to figure out what they are saying so that you can repeat it and sing along. There is a time to sing, and a time to listen. Distinguishing the difference between these anointings and ministry modes will allow people to experience much more of the fullness of what the Lord is releasing through musicians and singers in all of these realms.

The Contemporary Worship Leader

Worship Leader is the most commonly used term to describe those that lead sets of prewritten songs during the first part of a church meeting. In many churches, one common view of the worship portion of a meeting is that it is a primer to get the people ready for the preaching portion of the meeting. This viewpoint, in some cases, has reduced the worship portion of the meeting to become little more than a produced song service.

I recall leading worship for a three-night conference. The people were hungry for the presence of the Lord and each night the worship intensified as people continued to move in greater levels of expression. On the third night, the level of expectation was intense in the people. People were dancing with joy all over the place, enjoying their freedom in the presence of the Lord. The minister later took the service, did the announcements, took the offering and then said, "*Is everybody ready for what God is about to do tonight?*"

Honestly, I was surprised at what he said. My first thought was, "*What do you think that hour of praise and worship was, just a warm up?*" I personally think it's time to abolish this mentality that it's only time to hear the word of the Lord during the sermon. Music is not just a tool to be used to prepare people to hear the preaching of sermons. Musicians are not a prep crew. Through the musical skill and anointing that God has placed upon musicians, they have the ability to administer the word of God to others without even speaking.

In my case, when I have functioned in the role of "*worship leader*" in the church, I've often had to repress my unction to minister as a prophetic minstrel in order to do what leadership desired. I have led in churches where pastors literally told me to just sing the songs everyone knows and to not go off into the "*spontaneous stuff.*" Once a pastor even yelled at me from the front row in front of the whole church during the worship time! The church at large tends to create platforms that people are allowed to minister within. *"Oh, you sing and play an instrument; well you must be a 'worship leader.'"* The modern church, for the most part, does not have a platform yet for the minstrel, but it's coming.

My opinion is that the phrase Worship Leader is not as accurate a term as Worshipper Leader. I do not really lead worship, I lead worshippers. The point is not to lead songs; the point is to lead worshippers into an awareness of the presence of the Lord. I prefer not to be called a Worship Pastor because I do not pastor worship, I pastor people. Some may argue I bring up only an issue of semantics. The truth is that when a music minister begins to view his/her role as simply a song leader, a disconnecting with the people can oftentimes occur. I believe the goal is to lead people into the presence of God, not just in the singing of songs.

My observance is that in many modern-day church circles, people can often become familiar with a comfortable repertoire of songs. I once drove past a church with a sign that advertised their meeting with a banner that read, *"Thirty-Minute Worship."* People can become used to certain styles of music and durations of time so that whenever they are presented with something different, something that breaks the form, they become uncomfortable.

If you are comfortable, the possibility exists that you may not be growing. When I work out lifting weights, I am sometimes sore the next day. That uncomfortable feeling is a sign that something is happening. I pushed my body beyond what was comfortable. Over time, I will become comfortable with the weight that once made me sore, and I will have the option to press on even further. Sometimes you have to risk being uncomfortable in order to explore expanded places in the presence of God.

I define the term *worship leader* in this sub-chapter, not necessarily because I believe that it is the best phrase to define the calling of those with musical gifts in the church, but because that is the phrase that the modern church has used to describe and define musicians. The church tends to define things and set parameters, but what definition often ends up leading to is limitation. Definitions create expectations within people. When people hear the phrase *worship leader*, for the most part, they will base their definition of what they, through their experience, think a worship leader should look like and act like. When a musical minister begins to move into something that person is not used to, a wall goes up and they are unable to enter in. Consider with me that we may need to rethink and expand the definition and role of singers and musicians in the Body of Christ.

You need to know that my intention here is not to speak anything negative about the worship leader. But, especially in the context the modern Westernized church culture, I believe that the worship leader, in some cases, is only operating in PART of what God really desires for them to function in. I want to share this as an encouragement, but some may not receive it that way. To tell someone that they are only operating in part of what is their potential can either be received by the recipient as a put-down or encouragement to embrace a fuller operation of their gifts and calling. That said, I believe that any person that functions as a worship leader can, and should, also learn to function as a minstrel. In many churches today they do not.

For the most part, the worship leader puts together a list of songs to be sung for a worship service. Most of the time, the worship leader is singing songs that others have written, due to the fact that it's easier to lead people in what they have already known and have become familiar with.
Here is why I think a worship leader, **as they are generally defined**, is different from the psalmist and the minstrel. Most of what the worship leader does is lead others in singing revelations that other people have had. Songs are essentially rev-

elations that God gave people, which they put to music. Now worship has even become an industry in our nation, and that is part of why I believe that people are losing their personal expression.

I don't want you to think that I think it is wrong to lead songs in this way. I do think it is confining when people lean solely on the worship leader and prewritten songs to define for them who God is and how they will encounter His nature and character. If we lose our personal discovery because we rely on others to discover for us, we will miss some things that God desires for us to discover in a personal way. The function of the worship leader leading others in the repetition of second-hand musical revelations is a valid form of worship, but it is not THE ONLY WAY to do it. When any style or format becomes THE WAY, then we begin to miss out on the fullness of what God desires for us and from us.

The Psalmist

When I hear the term Psalmist I naturally think of David, the composer of a large portion of the Psalms. I believe that much of David's writing was inspired during times of solitude he experienced in the fields tending sheep. The Psalms are expressions from the heart of man to the Lord. The psalmist sings and/or plays before the Lord to glorify and praise Him for who He is and what He has done.

The ministry of the psalmist is the foundation upon which the ministry of the minstrel is laid. The prophetic word that I received was that I would function in the minstrel's anointing, but I did not function in that anointing right away. From the time I received that word, I did not really begin to function in the minstrel's anointing consistently until more than five years later. What was I doing during those years? I was functioning in my role as a psalmist. I spent hours in my worship room ministering to the Lord. It was during these times that I began to develop a deeper understanding of the heart of the Lord.

I believe that anyone called to function as a minstrel first needs to be established as a psalmist. That relationship to the Lord must grow and deepen. The ministry of the prophetic minstrel is simply the overflow of the exchange that takes place in the heart of the psalmist in relation to the Lord. Many times, when I have flowed in the minstrel's anointing, I received a word or song from the Lord days or even weeks before I released it publicly. As I see it, the psalmist's ministry is an ongoing preparation for the ministry of the minstrel. The psalmist's ministry is not a season, it is a lifestyle. We need to consistently be before the Lord, ministering to Him and receiving fresh words from His heart for ourselves and for those to whom we will minister. Although a psalmist may never step into a role as a minstrel, a minstrel should always, first and foremost, function as a psalmist.

The major difference between the psalmist and the minstrel is that the psalmist plays and sings unto God while the minstrel plays and sings on behalf of God. The psalmist releases personal expressions to the Lord while the minstrel's goal is to tune into the heart of God in order to release His expression to people.

There have been instances when I have been ministering to the Lord as a psalmist in a house of prayer and felt as if the people in attendance were watching my intimacy with God on display. As a psalmist, my priority is in ministering to God, not man. In this scenario, I would have much rather created an atmosphere, as a minstrel, for those people to have had their own personal encounter with the Lord. Yes, there will be times when others are encouraged by what I am seeing and releasing as a psalmist, but there is also a time when others need to see God as they need to see Him for their own lives.

The Psalmist's Release as a Minstrel

I've been involved in what many have dubbed the *"prayer movement"* for many years. I've seen countless houses of prayer spring up all over the United States and the world. I've helped establish houses of prayer and directed a house of prayer for a season in Dallas, TX. As a musician and singer myself, although I've enjoyed the house of prayer ministry of worship and prayer to the Lord as a psalmist, I've always had a calling to release music as a minstrel to minister to people as well.

In my past experience functioning as a psalmist, I was always releasing my heart to the Lord and receiving from His. For me it was not the place to release anything to anyone else, especially when most of the time there were not any other people in the prayer room anyway. When the Lord began to release me as a minstrel, I began to create atmospheres for others to encounter God through the music and the prophetic declaration that I released through music, word and song.

The psalmist's release into the function of a minstrel is not a *"graduation,"* but simply another form of manifesting the gift of music and song. I believe that houses of prayer, if they have not yet already, will began hosting venues in order to release the psalmists to minister and function as the prophetic minstrels of the Lord. There will be sessions and time slots that will be devoted towards ministering prophetically to the people that attend. I believe in the effectual power of prayer, and I believe that the Spirit of God can reach across time and space and touch the heart of anyone at anytime through prayer. That being said, I also believe that we've arrived to the time and place where these psalmists are going to be released into venues and platforms that will allow for their release into the minstrels' anointing and function for the purpose of ministering directly to people.

The Minstrel

2 Kings 3:15: *"But now bring me a minstrel. And it came to pass, when the minstrel played, that the hand of the Lord came upon him (Elisha), and he prophesied...."* (KJV)

This scripture is foundational in understanding the anointing and role of the minstrel as well as understanding the relationship between the minstrel and the prophetic ministry.

Although the Bible does not allude to Elisha calling for a minstrel at any other time in Scripture, I believe it is safe to assume that he had done so before. The relationship between Elisha and the minstrel was one of a partnership, joined for the purpose of hearing the thoughts and intents of the Lord. Elisha knew that when he called the minstrel forth that the anointing upon the musician would create an atmosphere conducive to hearing from the Lord. The prophetic word that Elisha went on to speak was brought forth in the musical atmosphere created by the minstrel. Of course, there will be times when the prophetic comes forth without the service of a minstrel. But it is apparent here that the minstrel is called to create atmospheres conducive to hearing the Lord and releasing the word of the Lord. In other words, when the minstrel creates, people have opportunity to start receiving from God!

David: Psalmist & Minstrel

David is the best example in recorded scripture of one who flowed in the ministry of both a psalmist and a minstrel. An example of David ministering as a psalmist can be realized in the entirety of Psalm 43:

"Vindicate me, O God, and plead my cause against an ungodly nation; rescue me from deceitful and wicked

men. You are God my stronghold. Why have you rejected me? Why must I go about mourning, oppressed by the enemy? Send forth your light and your truth, let them guide me; let them bring me to your holy mountain, to the place where you dwell. Then will I go to the altar of God, to God, my joy and my delight. I will praise you with the harp, O God, my God. Why are you downcast, O my soul? Why so disturbed within me? Put your hope in God, for I will yet praise him, my Savior and my God."

It is not at all out of the realm of possibility that David sang this Psalm as he played his harp. David grew up tending his father's sheep in the fields. He had a lot of time to spend with the Lord. It is during these years that David's heart grew as a worshipper and psalmist. It is apparent through many of the Psalms that David composed that he had a close and personal relationship with God. It was out of this place of intimacy with the Lord that he was anointed to minister to others. David flowed in such an anointing upon the harp that he actually began to gain a reputation in the land. How do we know this? Let's look at 1 Samuel 17:17–18, *"So Saul said to his attendants, 'Find someone who plays well and bring him to me.' One of the servants answered, 'I have seen a son of Jesse of Bethlehem who knows how to play the harp. He is a brave man and a warrior. He speaks well and is a fine-looking man. And the Lord is with him.'"*

Apparently the servant in this scripture had actually seen David play the harp before. I believe that David had already built up a reputation as a minstrel in the land. How else would this servant have known about him? Now, David was about to go from the sheep field to the palace. God was taking one of His psalmists and releasing David to minister as a minstrel to a man through the skill and the anointing that he had developed in the presence of the Lord.

1 Samuel 16:19-23: *"Then Saul sent messengers to Jesse and said, 'Send me your son David, who is with the sheep.' So Jesse took a donkey loaded with bread, a skin of wine and a young goat and sent them with his son David to Saul. David came to Saul and entered his service. Saul liked him very much, and David became one of his armor-bearers. Then Saul sent word to Jesse, saying, 'Allow David to remain in my service, for I am pleased with him.' Whenever the spirit from God came upon Saul, David would take his harp and play. Then relief would come to Saul; he would feel better, and the evil spirit would leave him."*

We see that David had the anointing, as a minstrel, to play the harp and create peaceful atmospheres in which King Saul was able to be at rest. Notice that it never says that David sang during these times, but only mentions that he played upon the harp. This is a prime example of a minstrel creating an atmosphere simply with instrumental music. David did not need to sing, "Be at peace." David had an understanding of how to tap into the peace of the Lord and represent that peace through the musical notes that he played. David's music exuded peace and all Saul had to do was enter in to the atmosphere that David was anointed to create.

Atmosphere Creators

Have you ever been to an art gallery and had a piece inspire you to the point where even your thoughts and emotions changed? Maybe it brought you joy and laughter, or possibly a sense of sadness accompanied by the shedding of a tear. In essence, that piece of art induced you into a personal atmosphere whereby, if only for a moment, you were changed and taken into a different state of mind than where you had been just moments before. The artist's intent is that those that experience their art would be taken into the experience and state of mind that he or she was in during the time that they created the piece.

This is the ability of an artist. They are able to create artistic renderings that evoke in others emotions and that even alter their states of being. There is a certain power in being an artist. Musicians are able to evoke physical movements from masses of people in unison. Just a simple uttering of, "*Wave your hands in the ayer. Wave 'em like you just don't cayer!*" can cause a frantic display of careless arm wavers during a music concert. With that creative power comes responsibility, and it is up to the individual artist whether or not they will use this gift to glorify the Lord.

Not all Minstrels Prophesy with Words

About six months after the initial prophetic word I received about the minstrel's anointing, I received a confirming word about this. A confirming word, as I define it, is a word that encourages you to know that you are on the right track. The specific way that the woman spoke over me was that I would be a "*prophet with a song.*" Basically, she was saying that the Lord would speak to others through songs that I would sing.

One important thing that I want to point out is that, even though I personally have a calling to both prophesy through music and singing, not all minstrels will necessarily speak or sing the prophetic word of the Lord. When the minstrel created an atmosphere for Elisha, it was Elisha who prophesied. I have functioned in this way before when I have created a musical atmosphere for another minister to speak the word of the Lord. There are also times where I will essentially create an atmosphere for myself to speak or sing the prophetic word of the Lord. This is when I function as a prophet with a song. I am simultaneously functioning both as a minstrel and a prophet. Again, not all minstrels will function in this capacity. The important thing is that the word of the Lord is heard. There will be times when I minister that I am led to simply play and encourage the people to listen for what the Lord is speaking.

It's important to me that I bring these points forth because there will be some that read this book who feel a calling to function as a minstrel without feeling as if they will necessarily sing or speak as they play. The minstrel is anointed to create an atmosphere in which all may perceive what the Lord is releasing. This does not necessarily mean that the minstrel is the one to release God's word verbally in every instance.

Minstrels Are God's Artists, Not Man's Entertainers

Although God's original intent was that the minstrels be artistic creators for His purposes, through time the minstrel's role morphed into that of an entertainer. From the 12th century to the 17th, the term minstrel defined a professional entertainer of any kind. Minstrels varied in operation from that of a juggler, acrobat, storyteller, or more specifically, a professional secular musician, usually an instrumentalist. They traveled from place to place; often living off the contributions of those they performed for.

I believe that we are seeing God's true purpose for the minstrel restored. In order to see this restoration, people will have to shift their mindsets from those of the entertained to those of participants. I believe that the original function of the minstrel was lost to entertainment because of people's desire and demand to be entertained. The minstrel creates an atmosphere, but in that place, people need to take a pro-active role in listening, hearing and acting upon what is heard.

People that expect to be entertained by the true prophetic minstrels will be disappointed because that is not the minstrel's role. The minstrel doesn't do entertainment. The minstrel is a catalyst whose role is to spur others on to revelation and creativity as they encounter the presence of the living God.

The minstrel's anointing is not just reserved for musical artists. I believe that all types of artists can function as a prophetic minstrel. Painters, sculptors, movers, dancers, singers, musicians, poets, writers, actors, film makers, graphic designers, photographers and more can all function in the anointing of the minstrel. The minstrel uses his/her artistic medium to evoke others in to the awareness of the person and presence of God. Their art is created with a purposeful intent that others, whether now or in the future, will be drawn to the nature, character and presence of the Lord as a result of their artistic expression.

Minstrels In History

History has shown that time often erodes the original purpose and intent for things and leaves us with something altogether different. This is true of God's purpose and intent for the minstrel. The original intent and purpose for the minstrel was one that would serve others by creating atmospheres that would lead them into the presence and perception of the Lord. In the Bible we see the minstrel flowing in these purposes. As history continues, we begin to see a shift occur in which the minstrel becomes less a representative of God and more an entertainer of man. It's important to understand God's original intent for the prophet musicians known as minstrels in order that, in our modern day, restoration can take place.

It is interesting to note the variety, throughout history, in which minstrels performed and the way in which the culture received them. Throughout history there were minstrels that entertained men, and yet there were those that continued to move in God's original intent as minstrels for the Lord. As we look into the history of the minstrel, let us begin with the history we find in the Word of God.

Samuel's Prophets with a Song

1 Samuel 10:5-6 *"After that you will go to Gibeah of God, where there is a Philistine outpost. As you approach the town, you will meet a procession of prophets coming down from the high place with lyres, tambourines, flutes and harps being played before them, and they will be prophesying. The Spirit of the Lord will come upon you in power, and you will prophesy with them; and you will be changed into a different person."*

Samuel is speaking to Saul in this Scripture. Here we see the power of God displayed through the prophetic musicians. When Saul came into the musical atmosphere that was created by these men, it says that the Lord changed Saul's heart. He was transformed into a different person as a result of being in that atmosphere.

History records that in the time of Samuel, there were men who followed him, praising God in song and attempting to call the people back to God. They had the gift and anointing to help others get on track with what God wanted to do in their lives. After Saul was anointed by Samuel, he was instructed to meet with these minstrels. There was a purpose in the meeting for Saul, and it was part of his preparation for the next season of his life as King. It is obvious that this experience had a lasting impact upon his life, as we see later that this is not the last time that Saul had interaction with a minstrel.

David

In 1 Samuel 16 we find the story of David in Saul's service as a minstrel. The word says that an evil spirit was tormenting Saul. It's an interesting thought to consider that Saul asked for someone who played the harp to come and play based on his prior experience with Samuel's musical prophets. Saul understood, based upon his past experience, the power of music played under the anointing of God. I am sure Saul remembered his experience with Samuel's company of prophets and believed that if it ministered to him before, it could minister to him now. This instance is an example of the minstrel creating an atmosphere where the peace of God manifests and overcomes the negative atmosphere that Saul was living under. To manifest the reality of His Kingdom is one of God's original intentions for music and the minstrel.

Elisha's Minstrel

In 2 Kings 3, Elisha called for a minstrel to play. As the minstrel played, the prophetic spirit of God came upon Elisha and he prophesied. This historical account reveals the ability of the minstrel to create atmospheres that help others tune into the voice of God. Elisha knew that the music released by the minstrel would aid him in focusing on what the Lord was saying.

Samuel's Minstrels Strike Again

1 Samuel 19:18-24 tells the story of Saul sending men to capture David. With Saul in pursuit, David had fled to Samuel who was accompanied by the company of prophet musicians that we first met back in 1 Samuel 10. Saul had

embraced jealousy and fear of David displacing him after he had gone against the instructions of Samuel the prophet. He sent three different sets of men to try to capture David, but each time a group of men would approach David's camp, they would begin to prophesy. After three tries, Saul himself decided to go and ended up prophesying all night in Samuel's presence. These men were attempting to capture David, but were stopped in their tracks due to the atmosphere that was created by the prophetic minstrels. I like to say that the minstrels created a *"musical force field."* This biblical account reveals the power of the minstrel's anointing to bring protection and shelter from evil intent.

God's Original Intent for the Minstrel

As we have looked at the minstrel through the historical lens of the Bible, we can deduce what God originally intended for the minstrel. Through Samuel's prophet musicians, we see that they had an anointing to create atmospheres that called people to the presence of God. It is in God's presence that Saul and others were changed. We also later see that they were used to create an atmosphere that brought protection and shelter to David from the evil intents of Saul's men. Through David's life we see that the minstrel has an anointing to create atmospheres for deliverance. And through the minstrel that Elisha called, we see the minstrel creating an atmosphere conducive to hearing what God was saying.

Through these passages of Scripture we can see that God originally intended the minstrel to be one who created musical atmospheres for revelation, deliverance and freedom. The minstrels used their gifts to call their society back to God. The minstrel was never to receive any glory for himself. In these times, the minstrel was never the source for anything, simply a conduit by which men and God connected.

The minstrel simply acted as a servant of men for the purpose of drawing them nearer to God.

The Minstrel's Shift Toward Entertainment

Entertainment creates a temporary sense of what only the presence of God can give us consistently. Throughout European and early American history, minstrels sought to bring entertainment to both esteemed royalty and the masses in order to soothe them away from the weights and trappings of life. God's intent is that we find our refuge in Him. In the presence of the Lord is where we find true, lasting peace and joy, but many have continued to seek out other sources for their contentment. We know that there are anti-Christian spirits in the earth, those that focus on engaging us in a constant array of distractions from knowing Jesus Christ. I think it is important to look into the history of secular minstrels and others who, through music, caused the minds of men to be drawn towards that which was not of Christ and His Kingdom. Looking into history to see the misuse of the function of the minstrel helps us learn and discover the ways in which the minstrel should truly function.

The European Minstrels

John Southworth gives a fantastic description of the minstrel in his book *The English Medieval Minstrel*:

The origin for the term Minstrel indicates that the minstrel was associated with a particular court. The old French word menestrel makes its first appearance as applied to an entertainer or musician. Its Latin root is ministrellus, meaning "a minor court official — a 'little servant' or 'minister' of the king; but with the secondary meaning of someone who practised a mestier or craft." In the middle of the thirteenth century, the word minstrel was chosen as a collective term that embraced all manner of professional performers of the day. This included composers, instrumentalists, singers, oral poets, taletellers, fools, jugglers, acrobats, dancers, actor, mimes, mimics, conjurors, puppeteers, and animal trainers. It was not until the sixteenth century that the term minstrel was used solely as a description for a musical performer. Others forms of performance acquired their own description again such as players, jesters, clowns and tumblers.[1]

For the most part, the minstrels served as entertainers both in the royal courts and as traveling street performers. The minstrels of this era were professionals in the sense that they depended for their livelihood — if not exclusively, primarily — on their performing skills. It is interesting to note that the minstrel was defined as a little servant. Even though the minstrel was more of an entertainer, he was still defined as one who served others by way of their gifts.[2]

Many minstrels had incredible relationships with the royalty of their day. The minstrels were representatives of the King and his Kingdom. The songs the minstrels played in the city streets were essentially paid advertisements for the Kingdom.

When the minstrels went touring, they did so on their own or in groups. When they went alone, they went out as *"The King's Harper"* or *"The King's Piper."* When they went as a group they were collectively known as *"The King's Minstrels."* These minstrels were trusted servants and companions of the King. Their functions as entertainers were secondary to that or rather, was an aspect of their relationship — and may sometimes have been combined with other services such as watchmen, messengers or wayfarers.[3]

I like to say that I function just like the European

Minstrels of old, except that I represent a different King and a different Kingdom. Not unlike the function of the European Minstrels, the function of God's Minstrels is also secondary to their relationship to the King. The Minstrels of the Lord are coming out of His throne room, going forth to decree the songs of His Kingdom to the earth. They are His musical messengers.

The Celtic Bards

Many native cultures either had no written language or, if they did, had only a few people in the community that were able to record the history of the people. Many cultures used singing and storytelling as a means of preserving the legends and tales of the cultural history and ancestry.

In the book Celts, Aedeen Cremin writes, *"People with a short life span and who do not use writing have a very restricted memory, both of the history of their own families and of their group. This was overcome in practice by a strong oral tradition with an emphasis on poetry, which celebrated the history of individual families. Each Celtic chief had a resident poet bard, whose job it was to memorize and recite the highlights of the chief's life and that of his ancestors."* [4]

These bards essentially kept the stories of their forefathers alive by bringing their deeds to remembrance through the poetry, music and the arts. It helped people to not only remember who their ancestors were, but it also stirred within them afresh who they were as well.

I have often been in meetings where I would begin to declare the attributes of who God is. It begins to stir people back to the knowledge of who their God is, and it also stirs them to a fresh acknowledgement of who they are in the power of their Father. We need the *"Kingdom of God Bards"* to be released in order that they may continue to release afresh, not just the memories of who God was and what He did, but also who He is in us and how His power is alive and active in our present situations. The *"Bards of God"* will release encouragement to the church and the earth. Their songs will bring hope, light and Kingdom perspective to dark situations.

Saint Francis of Assisi — Troubadour & Jester of God

We've spent time looking into the lives of secular minstrels and bards. Now I want to focus upon one man in history who rediscovered God's Kingdom intent for the minstrel, Saint Francis of Assisi. Saint Francis is well known for his quote, *"Preach the Gospel at all times and, when necessary, use words."* Although I had been familiar with this quote for many years, it brought new meaning to me once I began to look into the life of Saint Francis, the musician. I believe that Saint Francis used the music he played and the countenance of his face to speak as strongly as his words did.

Let me interject and introduce another word to you, troubadour. A troubadour was in essence the French version of a minstrel. Francis was a troubadour who fashioned himself after the French poets who would travel the countryside and sing their courtly songs of love. Francis is quoted as saying, *"After I began to follow Jesus, my musical muse didn't dry up and die. Instead, the music I created began to reflect my newfound faith. Where before I had railed like an angry prophet against racism, militarism and environmental degradation, my new spiritual perspective helped me to see that these social ills were all aspects of our separation from God."*[5]

After Francis began to imitate the life of Jesus, he too incorporated his creative spark into his new life. The man who had once paraded through the streets of Assisi singing the songs of the troubadours now traveled through the same streets with a group of singing friars. Francis called this new band the *"jongleurs de Dieu."* The man who once belted out songs of chivalric and courtly love now spread the joy of God by becoming a *"Jester of God."*

Saint Francis and the Lord's Minstrels

The first Franciscan convent was formed by the erection of a few small huts or cells of wattle, straw, and mud, and enclosed by a hedge. From this settlement, which became the cradle of the Franciscan Order and the central spot in the life of St. Francis, the Friars Minor went forth two by two exhorting the people of the surrounding country. Like children *"careless of the day,"* they wandered from place to place singing in their joy, and calling themselves the *"Lord's Minstrels."* They traveled the countryside sleeping in haylofts, grottos or church porches. In a short time Francis and his companions gained an immense influence, and men of different grades of life and ways of thought flocked to the Order.[7]

Saint Francis and the Healing Power of Music

In his later life, Francis dealt with sickness but history records his belief in the healing power of God through music. One day Francis was staying in the town of Rieti. As was often the case, some of those around Francis at the time were musicians and artists. Suffering from a variety of physical ailments, the saint asked a brother who had worked as a musician before joining the Franciscan movement to play his zither to ease his pain.[8] Francis wanted music and song even when he was dying. He asked his brother friars to praise God with him by singing the Canticle of the Creatures which he had composed while he was ill and going blind. He used to say, moreover, that he wanted his friars to go about the world like minstrels to *"inspire the hearts of people and stir them to spiritual joy."* [9]

We Need the Minstrels Today

Let me be straight with you here by saying that I in no way believe that the function of the minstrel is THE WAY that God is going to speak to the church and the earth in the coming days, but I do believe it is A WAY. Just as Francis and his company traveled throughout the countryside of France, minstrels are being released in our time for the purpose of releasing God's Kingdom truth to the hearts of people all across the earth. Having an understanding of the minstrel will help the Body of Christ receive them, not as entertainers, but as the conduits of the Kingdom of the Lord that they are.

---

[1] John Southworth, *The English Medieval Minstrel* (Woodbridge: Boydell and Brewer, 1989), 3.

[2] Ibid., 4.

[3] Ibid., 64.

[4] Aedeen Cremin, *The Celts* (Rizzoli International Publications, 2000), 16.

[5] John Michael Talbot, *The Lessons of St. Francis* (Penguin, 1998), 95-96.

[6] Ibid., 96

[7] Padre Pio, The Franciscan. Retrieved October 19, 2011 from http://www.ewtn.com/padrepio/franciscan/st_francis4.htm

[8] John Michael Talbot, op. cit.,100.

[9] Friar Jack. Muses on a dozen red roses. Retrieved October 17, 2011 from http://www.americancatholic.org/e-News/FriarJack/fj070802.asp

Chapter Nine
The Ministry of the Minstrel

In this final chapter, I want to share some insights into the vision, purpose and function of our ministry. I have shared previously how, over the course of years in ministry, I began recognizing a theme of refreshing in our meetings. I began to understand that my purpose for traveling and ministering was to create atmospheres for people to be renewed in their bodies, minds and spirits in the presence of the Lord. Out of this realization the Lord gave me the word *Rejuvenation* which means to restore to a former state. I love this because God is a re-creator and restorer. Our desire is to connect with others relationally across the nations for the purpose of traveling to share the insights that you have just read and to create musical atmosphere for people to be rejuvenated in the presence of the Lord.

God's Kingdom Reporters

God revealed to me that one of my roles, as a prophetic minstrel, is to see into the realm of the Spirit, the realm of His Kingdom, and to report what I'm seeing to others. Sometimes these reports are corporate while sometimes the report God reveals is a specific thing for a specific person in the midst of a gathering. You see, people leave our meetings rejuvenated, not simply because the music was good, but because they got re-aligned with the sound and vibration of God's Kingdom. I am a *"Kingdom Reporter"* that assists people to hear and align themselves with what God is speaking. There is a need for this in society right now. We can get so distracted to the point that we don't even realize how out of tune we are.

There is a Heavenly Kingdom that is greater than all of the kingdoms of the earth. God desires us to live life tuned according to the words that He has already spoken and established. This is what it means to live the supernatural life, a life that supersedes the natural. There are avenues of being healed, being provided for and being directed in life that are accessible beyond the scope of what we sense in what is called the natural spectrum. The vibration of the sound of God's word in our spirits needs to be maintained or it will either grow silent or be taken over by a negative vibration. All of us need to be continually under the sound of God's word so that His re-sounding word will be maintained within us.

God is releasing *"Musical Kingdom Reporters"* that will travel to the nations to release the realities of the Kingdom of God. These sounds and songs will take precedence over the sounds and songs of the kingdoms of the earth. It may not necessarily change what is happening in the government or economy, at least not right away. But it will change the thoughts and intents of the hearts of men and women that desire to keep their minds stayed upon Jesus and His Word. What you allow to resound within you will eventually be released in the way you live your life and carry yourself.

What I Do and How I Do It

I want share with you how I actually minister when I travel to various venues. If I had to choose one word that describes how I begin a time of ministry, it would be *"scanning."* When I sit down to a piano, besides having a few chord charts picked out, I really don't have much of an idea what I am about to do. Some may call this poor planning. I think it's a great plan! My plan is to scan for God's plan and then release it the best way I can through music and sound.

When I play my instrument, I am not just creating an atmosphere for the people gathered but for myself as well. I will usually spend time just playing and *"scanning in the Spirit."* When I am scanning in the Spirit I am simply putting my antenna out to pick up on any kind of frequency that the Lord is releasing in the moment. There are times when my spirit acts like a radio and sometimes like a television. Sometimes God's signal comes in the form of a sound and sometimes in the form of a picture. When I hear a sound I relay that sound through music or song. When I see a picture I sing or speak a description of what I am seeing in my *"spirit's eye."*

In a recent meeting, while I was playing and scanning, I saw a picture of a frustrated man driving a car and I knew the car was related to this man's job. Through this picture I knew that a man in the crowd was frustrated with his job as a driver and was seeking the Lord for new direction with his career. I began to sing out this vision and spoke encouragement that the Lord knew this man's situation and that God wanted this man to turn his car into a moving prayer closet. After the meeting a limo driver came up to me and told me that this word was for him.

When I was ministering in Prague, a man on the church's ministry team approached me and asked me to pray for him. He told me that he purposefully did not want to share what was going on in his life and that he wanted me to simply pray what the Lord would put upon my heart. I put my hand on his shoulder and simply waited in silence for a few minutes. While I waited before the Lord, in my *"spirit's eye"* I saw a large sheet of paper being torn in two. The Lord spoke to me that this man was being torn between his job as an international businessman and his desire for ministry. I spoke this over him and asked God for clarity in his life. After our prayer together, he told me that out of all the things I could have prayed, this was the issue that was heaviest upon his heart. This same man spent the next summer ministering.

This is how I seek God in my own life. Sometimes I play music while other times I take a walk or sit in silence. There are times when I receive a large vision; other times I get the next piece of a large puzzle. One thing I've learned is that I cannot control what I receive; I can only control my side of the coin, which is listening, waiting and scanning. There are times when the Lord prompts me to release what I am receiving, while other times the Lord tells me to be silent so that people can pick up on what He Himself is transmitting to the people as individuals.

There are times when God lays a song on my heart to sing that brings people back to a place of adoration before the Lord. Sometimes they are well-known songs and sometimes they are choruses that we create in the moment.

I love ministering this way because no meeting is ever like the previous one. When I travel to different regions of the United States, I will often sense different things in people based on the culture and conditions in which they are living in. It's important to me to be able to tap into where people are. I want them to get in touch with the things God desires to speak to them for the moment they are living in. That's why I don't heavily rely upon songs that were created out of circumstances that don't relate to where people are at or what they are going through. Sometimes I will remember a song that applies and sing it with the people, but there are times when we all just create our own songs in the moment. **The reality of the diversity of people's current experiences is what makes creating neutral musical atmospheres so valuable and practical.** It allows people to essentially create their own download center in the midst of a corporate meeting where they can both receive from God and release unto God.

What I do is as simple as waiting, scanning, perceiving and releasing. This is how I function in the context of a prophetic music venue. It requires confidence and trust that the Lord will manifest and reveal His heart. But, if you trust His word that you will find Him when you seek Him, there should be no doubt. Honestly, everyone that functions in this type of ministry should have already done so numerous times in their own walk with God. When I minister, I am simply living out my walk with the Lord in the context of a corporate gathering and sharing my spiritual gifts with others so that they can encounter the Lord personally as well.

Rejuvenation Gatherings

I have been building relationships with leaders in the Body of Christ for a number of years. As one who is called to travel and minister in different locations, it's been vitally important to build relationships with others in different regions of the United States and in the nations as well.

A Rejuvenation Gathering is something that we have implemented locally here in our home region of Dallas, TX and in others cities and states as well. We've held these meetings in various places from churches, to homes, to coffee shops and more. The purpose of this gathering is to offer a venue where people can come to engage into the presence of the Lord for the purpose of encouragement, exhortation, healing, and inspiration. It's a time where people can get away from the noise of life to engage into the presence of the Lord to be realigned with His Word.

One of the things the Lord graces me with is the ability to tune into what is going on spiritually in the different places that I travel. People are not going through the same things in Maine as they are in Texas or in New York City. When Paul the Apostle traveled, he also had sensitivity to what needed to be addressed to the churches of different regions. If this were not the case, he would have just written the same letter to all of the churches.

God wants to release His current testimony over the peoples of the earth to counter and overcome the noise that is released from pop culture, media, society and other negative sources. When I travel into a city or region, I am there to create an atmosphere for the release of the word of God so that people can come back into alignment with what the Spirit of the Lord is saying to the church.

During a recent gathering, my violinist friend Paula was tuning her instrument before the meeting started. The Lord spoke to me that our ministry is like a tuning session for people. If each of us is an instrument, life often *"plays us"* to the point that we end up out of whack and out of tune. We all need opportunities to enter into an atmosphere that allows for us to be tuned back into the place God intends for us. Our ministry is dedicated to creating environments, not where people can escape from their issues, but where they can encounter the One whose character holds the answer to their needs.

"Healing Man" Music

I've previously received, and continue to receive, prophetic words that healing will occur in the midst of the atmospheres that my team and I create. To me personally, the most significant of these prophetic words regarding this manifestation of healing is found right in the meaning of my name. In the sixth grade I did a family-tree project for my social studies class. While researching for this, my Grandpa Heilman told me that our last name meant, *"sound, healthy, healing man."* I also learned that the meaning of my first name is *"healer."* My name has prophesied and continues to prophesy that God will use me as His conduit to be a *"Healer Healing Man."* (By the way, it's no accident that many prophetic musicians that are currently being released in a healing anointing share my first name.)

The Lord has stirred my heart regarding creating musical venues for healing of both the physical body and the soul. At one of our Rejuvenation Conferences in Dallas, I coordinated teams of minstrels for the purpose of coming together on a Saturday to create a twelve-hour continual flow of prophetic music and declaration. The purpose for creating this extended time of ministry was to give people an opportunity to come and posture themselves under this flow of God's Word and Sound in order to be rejuvenated into alignment with His Word and Kingdom Reality.

One of the musicians that I asked to be a part of the event played for the first hour of the day. After she completed her time slot, I noticed that she stayed in the room for the entire rest of the day. She spent time resting and soaking in the manifest presence of God. Later that week my wife told me that this same girl had been healed of a sprained ankle on the day of the event that we hosted. She told my wife that by the end of the day she no longer sensed any pain in her ankle.

This is not the first time that someone has testified to being healed in one of our meetings. We have had other reports of both physical healing and emotional healing during extended times spent exposed to the music ministry that we were releasing.

What takes places during these times of *"sound ministry"* is that the people who spend time exposed to the sound are literally being brought back into resonance with the reality of God's Word on a cellular level. The sound literally repairs the body and soul. Understand that you were made and are destined to resonate with God and His Kingdom on subatomic levels. I believe that any disease, physical or emotional, can potentially shift back into alignment with God's good intent when the disease is exposed to the reality of God's Kingdom Sound. I don't play the music that I play with a desire that it be cool, edgy, relevant or popular. I play the sounds that I play with a desire to re-present the Kingdom

Sounds that will realign the diseased sounds of the human body and soul back into alignment with their destined resonance, the resonance of the reality of God's Word.

What happened that Saturday to that girl was her ankle was realigned with the Greater Reality. She remained under a continual, Kingdom of God sound over the course of the day, and in that place the disease of her ankle came under the influence of the Kingdom Sound at a cellular level. Over the course of the day, all that was not aligned with God's Kingdom Reality BECAME ALIGNED.

My desire is to bring this *"Healing Man"* music to the nations of the earth. God desires that we understand that music's purpose is for much more than our entertainment. His music, His sound can literally keep us aligned with His purpose and intent for us body, soul and spirit!

Networking and Equipping Musicians

I have a desire to see what we are doing with Rejuvenation Gatherings spring forward into the development of similar gatherings all across the USA and the nations. These gatherings can be hosted in any number of venues.

I desire to equip musicians with the realization and understanding of their ability to function in the anointing of a minstrel. We are believing to see hundreds of musicians, as well as other artists, equipped and released in the minstrel's anointing all across the earth. We are currently forming a coalition across the nation with churches, ministries and houses of prayer for the purpose of sharing how to practically facilitate gatherings like Rejuvenation into what they are already doing. Like I've previously shared, I believe it's time to equip and release musicians into the calling and function of the minstrel in their respective regions and spheres of influence.

Rejuvenation Missions

I was attending a Sunday morning service at our home church when a visiting missionary was introduced to the congregation. This missionary proceeded to tell us about the financial blessing that he had received that allowed him to fly halfway across the world from Eastern Europe to be refreshed. I was happy that he was there, but I was also re-ignited with a desire for what I call *"Missionary Missions."* Missionary Missions is traveling to a nation to minister to the missionaries themselves.

This missionary shared with us how burned out he and his congregation were back in Europe. He described how draining it can be when you are a Christian living within a nation of very few Christians. Like I said, I was glad that he was able to be with us, but it left me with a desire to take a team of prophetic minstrels to his church, city and nation.

I have a vision to take teams of prophetic minstrels out to minister to missionary families, their teams and their churches for the purpose of encouraging, rejuvenating and inspiring them in the presence of the Lord. It's a different perspective of what short-term missions can be. Honestly, most short-term mission teams actually create more work for missionaries because the missionaries have to host teams and create venues in which they can minister. There is nothing wrong with this, but my desire is to equip and take teams out for the purpose of bringing refreshing to the people that actually live and minister in the nations. I want to see teams of prophetic minstrels create venues for missionaries to receive renewed vision for what they are doing. We all deal with burnout from time to time. The fire that once initially blazed within us can often grow cold amongst the realities of life. As a short-term missionary, I can only have so much influence upon a people, society and culture over the course of a week or two. But, if I am able to help strengthen those that have, over years of work, built a respect and reputation in their culture, it will have a greater impact through them over the long run. We need to realize that sometimes we are called to work and sometimes we are called to support and strengthen others who are working.

As I previously described, this aspect of missions developed out of us being who God called us to be while we were in other nations ministering. I believe that Rejuvenation Missions Teams will increase in going forth to encourage missionaries all across the earth. Rather than missionaries having to raise funds and further drain themselves with extended travel to retreat to their home churches, I believe it's time for the minstrels to go forth in purpose and anointing to bring the refreshing to the workers.

Another way in which missions is accomplished by the prophetic minstrel is in a responsive way. I can remember when I was leading worship at a college ministry in Fort Worth, TX. The church I was ministering in was actually providing shelter for some Hurricane Katrina refugees that were in from Louisiana. I remember having a desire to hold a concert for these people, but not a concert of entertainment. It would be a concert to bring them to a place of peace in the presence of the Lord. When tragedy strikes, it's often a time of doubt, anger and confusion for those involved. I wanted to sing over them that God was for them and not against them. I wanted to seek and sing the song of the Lord that He wanted to sing over His children in the moment of their need. I believe that teams of prophetic minstrels will be released to places in the earth in response to cultural, ecological and governmental issues in order to release and establish Kingdom of God realities back into the hearts and minds of the people.

The 2011 Joplin, MO tornado was a devastating EF5 multiple-vortex tornado that struck late in the afternoon of Sunday, May 22, 2011. When I heard about this devastating event, I immediately began praying about how I might eventually go to Joplin to minister in the exact way that I had felt I wanted to minister to those Katrina refugees in Fort Worth. After praying, I felt led to call the director of a house of prayer in Joplin. What resulted is that I eventually led a team of musicians to Joplin for three days. We set up a tent right in the middle of the tornado damage path and ministered through music, prayer and the prophetic over the course of that weekend.

Prior to going, we held a benefit concert in order to raise funds for the team. Due to the generous help of our partners, we were able to go as an entire team to Joplin with all of our needs met. We responded to this tragedy as a team of prophetic minstrels and travelled to Joplin, MO to, just as Saint Francis' minstrels did in their historical time and place, *"inspire the hearts of people and stir them to spiritual joy."*

For me personally, standing on a dusty hill playing music in a tent overlooking a city is probably one of the most precise representations of the calling on my life as a prophetic minstrel that I can think of. As we released our songs and sounds, with the distant hum of the gas-powered generator in the background, I really don't think I could have felt more *"in the pocket"* of what I feel I was made to be and to do.

Kingdom Connections

As the traveling minstrels of God begin to emerge, it's a desire of my heart to be an example of how churches and leadership can build relationships and relate to those truly called to travel from place to place as God's *"Musical Messengers."*

The purpose of these relationships is for much more than churches providing venues for musicians to hold concerts. These relationships are Kingdom relationships that advance what God is doing in churches, cities and regions. When I travel to different places, my prayer is that I may join in with the Kingdom purposes God has for that place. I'm there to serve the Body of Christ to push forward into their specific destinies in God. Both my wife and I look forward to the many Kingdom connections that the Lord has in store for us!

About Jason & Ann-Marie

Jason and Ann-Marie Heilman are the founders of Heilman Ministries, Rejuvenation Music Gatherings and Movementology Dance Seminars. They travel extensively throughout the United States and the nations ministering through music, movement and teaching.

Jason operates in the calling and anointing of the prophetic musician and minstrel. The desire of Jason's heart is to serve the Body of Christ by creating "Musical Atmosphere" in which people can gather to hear what the Spirit of the Lord is saying. Through his understanding of music and sound, Jason is anointed to assist others to position and posture themselves before God, enabling them to tune more fully in to the frequency of the Kingdom of Jesus Christ. Through Jason's music and teaching ministry, people consistently receive divine revelation, encouragement, refreshing, direction and healing in the presence of God. Jason is a graduate of Christ for the Nations Institute Dallas, TX.

Ann-Marie is a professional movement artist and instructor with a diverse background, giving her unique insight into the mover's body. Ann-Marie began her training with Royal Academy of Fine Arts connected with the Clear Lake Metropolitan Ballet, then went on to Kilgore College to be a Rangerette Officer and Swingster. Afterwards, she attended Texas Christian University where she received her BFA in Modern Dance. Ann-Marie currently dances with Contemporary Dance/Fort Worth, a professional modern dance company, and serves on the staff of Dance Revolution and the Ingredients Training Program and Company. She is also the creator of Movementology, a teaching seminar and moving experience based on the theology of movement.

Jason and Ann-Marie currently reside in Dallas, TX with their beautiful daughter, Zoey Kulani.

Ministry Resources & Information

Rejuvenation Gathering
A one-night gathering focused on prophetic worship and declaration through music, song, movement and creative arts with the purpose of bringing an atmosphere of refreshing, revelation and healing to your church, home, business, missionary team or ministry.

Rejuvenation Conferences & Retreats
An extended Rejuvenation Gathering with added teaching and activation sessions. Teaching will focus on venturing more expansively into the presence of the Lord in atmospheres of prophetic music, worship, movement and artistic revelation. These teaching times can potentially be focused specifically towards musicians and artists, worshipers as a whole, or both depending upon what best serves your ministry's needs.

Book Reading & House Concert with Jason
Host Jason for an incredible evening of fellowship, sharing and music. After a time of socializing together, Jason will take to the microphone and share some brief book excerpts, followed by a time of music and worship in the intimate setting of the host home.

Movementology Dance Seminar with Ann-Marie
Delve with Ann-Marie into scriptural, cultural, and scientific research to understand why movement is close to the heart of God and is an important part of His Kingdom. Movementology will help you learn how to release your movement to the Lord and to receive the ministry of movement from others through teaching and exercises in which all ages and levels of movers can engage. Visit www.movementology.com for more information.

Prophetic Music & the Minstrel Seminar with Jason
This seminar is specifically geared to instruct singers and musicians how to flow in the anointing of the prophetic minstrel. Students will learn how to scan in the spirit, re-present the Kingdom Sound in their music, sing the song of the Lord and much more. This seminar focuses heavily upon the teachings shared in chapters 7-9 of Jason's book, The Potential of God's Presence.

You may also consider Jason for your next conference or event as a worshipper leader and/or guest speaker. Jason is a dynamic speaker and often uses humorous stories and anecdotes to bring spiritual principles into terms anyone can understand.

Inviting Jason & Ann-Marie

Our preferred initial ministry contact is through email:
contact@jasonheilman.com

Please send in your email a description of your ministry request, the preferred date(s) and time(s) for ministry, your desired goal for the ministry time, your contact information and any questions you may have. Someone will contact you shortly to begin the practical steps necessary towards the gathering.

Heilman Ministries does not require an up-front, set financial amount from a host ministry leader, host church, host missions organization or host ministry. We do budget and set financial goals for each gathering/seminar and we will share these goals with the host prior to the gathering(s). Again, these are the financial goals that need to be met for travel expenses and ministry operations. As the host, we simply ask that you prayerfully join us and assist us in meeting the practical needs and requirements of travel ministry through offerings and/or seminar registrations.

www.jasonheilman.com
www.movementology.com
www.thepotentialofgodspresence.com

Jason Heilman Music

I Can't Wear This Armor

This album represents the passion in Jason's heart to see God's people release their intimate, homemade Tehillah praises unto the Lord. This LIVE recording will draw you into places of expression & solitude in which you can engage into the person and presence of God. There is an awakening taking place in God's people to first-hand discovery of God and the release of first-hand worship expression from that place of discovery. Just as David dropped Saul's armor to the ground to be free to use what God gave him, many will drop their armor of religious formula in order to take up what God gave them in order to worship Him in spirit and in truth.

This Is The Generation

This Is The Generation is a collection of songs that have been birthed directly out of Jason's personal journey with Christ. More than just a collection of songs, these are prophetic words set to music that will encourage you on your personal journey.

Hear O Israel

Hear O Israel is a live, raw, "off the board" worship & intercession album recorded during the Uncommon Love Conference at Shady Grove Church. This album contains live versions of some of Jason's most well loved songs such as Fear God, Come Fall In Love and the album title song, Hear O Israel. This album is currently available on the ministry website as a free download.

All Jason Heilman Music is available for preview & purchase at www.jasonheilman.com and the iTunes Music Store

Join the Heilman Ministries Partner Community With Your Monthly Financial Support

Dear Friends,

By now you've read my words and perhaps been previously impacted by a message I've spoken, a song I've sung or a dance my wife has released. I pray you've come to see the value of what Ann-Marie and I do in ministry. Realize that, as a part of our Partners Community, you become a major part of what enables us to continue impacting and touching lives with the musical, moving message of the Kingdom. I understand that not every one of you will feel led to join us in monthly partnership at this time. But, if you feel a leading, I would graciously like to ask that you join us for a time period of monthly financial partnership for any amount that the Holy Spirit speaks to you. Realize that any piece, large or small, matters in the big picture.

There is a synergistic power released when you join and support what we are doing. I view each member of our partner community like an individual brick in a fortified wall joint together for Kingdom purposes. It's not just about Ann-Marie and I; it's about all of us. Your partnership will allow us increased time and enabling resource to continue doing what God has mandated us to do for His Kingdom.

Please consider becoming a part of this community and share in what God is doing in and through Heilman Ministries in the United Sates and the nations of the earth. For more detailed information, please take a look at our website www.jasonheilman.com and click on "partner with us." Once there, you will find information on how to partner with us monthly either online or via mail. Currently we stream our monthly support through our affiliate financial ministry, Modern Day. Modern Day exists to "build bridges between those who are called to go into all the world and those who are called to send them." All of your financial support is tracked and accounted for through Modern Day and you will receive monthly and yearly statements of your giving.

Blessings and thanks to you as you consider joining us,

Jason & Ann-Marie Heilman

We Want To Hear From You
Staying In Touch With Heilman Ministries

We want to hear your testimony of how this book has impacted your life. Please contact us by email and send us your personal review of *The Potential of God's Presence*. Your reviews are important to us; some will even be used in future blog posts and updates.

Email us at contact@jasonheilman.com

Stay informed with ministry happenings as well as Jason and Ann-Marie's travel schedule by joining our mailing list.

You can do so at www.jasonheilman.com

Jason has always been an active blogger, sharing teachings, podcasts, music and more. Subscribe to Jason's Wordpress Blog, *The Prophetic Sound Man*.

www.propheticsoundman.wordpress.com

You can also connect with Jason on his Facebook author page where you'll find current info and event listings.

www.facebook.com/authorjasonheilman

www.ingramcontent.com/pod-product-compliance
Lightning Source LLC
Chambersburg PA
CBHW052021290426
44112CB00014B/2329